FEDERAL
BUDGET
DEFICITS

FEDERAL BUDGET DEFICITS

America's Great Consumption Binge

Paul N. Courant
Edward M. Gramlich

Department of Economics
Institute of Public Policy Studies
The University of Michigan

Prentice-Hall, Inc., Englewood Cliffs, New Jersey 07632

Library of Congress Cataloging-in-Publication Data

Courant, Paul N.
    Federal budget deficits.

    Includes bibliographical references and index.
    1. Budget deficits—United States.   I. Gramlich,
Edward M.   II. Title.
HJ2051.C7 1986   339.5′23′0973   85-12218
ISBN 0-13-308438-8

Printed in the United States of America

10 9 8 7 6 5 4 3 2 1

Editorial/production supervision: Joe O'Donnell
Cover design: Ben Santora
Cover cartoon by Don Martinetti
Manufacturing buyer: Ed O'Dougherty

Much of the material in Chapter 5 was taken from the authors'
"The Expenditure Tax: Has the Idea's Time Finally Come,"
in J. Pechman et al., *Tax Policy: New Directions and Possibilities,*
Center for National Policy, Washington, D.C., 1985.

ISBN 0-13-308438-8   01

PRENTICE-HALL INTERNATIONAL (UK) LIMITED, *London*
PRENTICE-HALL OF AUSTRALIA PTY. LIMITED, *Sydney*
PRENTICE-HALL CANADA INC., *Toronto*
PRENTICE-HALL HISPANOAMERICANA, S.A., *Mexico*
PRENTICE-HALL OF INDIA PRIVATE LIMITED, *New Delhi*
PRENTICE-HALL OF JAPAN, INC., *Tokyo*
PRENTICE-HALL OF SOUTHEAST ASIA PTE. LTD., *Singapore*
EDITORA PRENTICE-HALL DO BRASIL, LTDA., *Rio de Janeiro*
WHITEHALL BOOKS LIMITED, *Wellington, New Zealand*

We dedicate this book to Helene C. McCarren, who in her subtle way made it all possible.

CONTENTS

PREFACE

The question economists are most often asked—by their fathers, mothers-in-law, uncles, and students—is about budget deficits. Why are they run, how can they be good, and why are government deficits any different from "my own" budget, which must be in balance? A first answer, often sufficient to deflect the attack at a cocktail party, is that one's own budget may not be in balance as often as one thinks. Rare, indeed, is the uncle who does not have some loans outstanding, who is not adding to those loans by running up his VISA balance at that very minute.

But apart from this glib deflection, there is a serious side to the question. For nearly sixty years, most economists have been arguing the dovish position on budget deficits: Deficits have usually not been large, they are devilishly difficult to measure properly in any case, and sometimes deficits are desirable. In recent years, however, much of that has been changed. Deficits are still difficult to measure properly, but now they are fairly large, they appear to be growing, and they do not appear to be desirable. And they appear to be harmful for reasons that are fairly subtle, because their real costs are pretty hard to observe.

This all means that, although the usual gut reaction people have against deficits is appropriate, it is rarely for the right reason. The usual arguments made against deficits—households cannot run them, they ruin the government's credibility, they cause excessive money creation, they cause inflation, they lead to collapses—are all either incorrect or misleading in most cases. The statement that all deficits are bad is clearly incorrect. Because sometimes deficits are bad and sometimes they are not, it becomes important to develop one's identification skills. How should a deficit be measured, how does one tell a good one from a bad one, and how does one know why some deficits are good and some are bad? Our goal here is to answer all of these questions.

We must give two caveats. Economics is, after all, a social science. Economic models are precise within their assumptions, but their assumptions never correspond exactly with reality. There is an important value to simplifying reality so that important truths can be learned, but reasonable people will disagree about the simplifications that should be made. Moreover, to analyze the impact of changes in budgetary totals on the economy requires some estimation of how households and firms will respond to these changes. Very often, there is doubt about the strength of certain behavioral responses, and that makes it difficult to predict impacts. Hence, there is often disagreement about the questions we deal with here, and we must often state things in a way that seems very cautious.

A second caveat concerns the writing. We have tried to talk to a lay audience and to make things as clear and free of jargon as possible. We have used appendices to illustrate some of the harder points, and we have even included a glossary that explains a few technical terms used in the book. With these aids, we are convinced that most of the main text can be understood by people with no previous training in economics. But there remain a few dark corners that will be difficult to penetrate for those with no prior training.

ACKNOWLEDGMENTS

Many have helped us in writing the book. As the dedication suggests, our biggest debt is to Helene McCarren, who keeps the Institute of Public Policy Studies running smoothly, no matter who is director. Without Helene's skill, neither of us would have had the time to write the book. Right behind Helene comes Deborah Laren, who provided consistently competent and careful management of our simulations, calculations, tables, charts, and references. Sharon Gennis-Deich also provided invaluable assistance in these areas. Finally, we are grateful to students in our seminar on fiscal policy at IPPS and to other faculty members in the program for providing both intellectual and material suggestions as we developed the ideas in the book.

We benefited from comments on the manuscript by Christopher Baum, Robert Heilbroner, Walter Heller, Jerry Miner, Joseph Pechman, and Murray Weidenbaum. We received added help in making things clear from Ruth Gramlich and Marta Manildi, who are used to translating our contorted arguments. And although modern-day microcomputers have spared others the agony of reading our illegible handwriting, computers and their printers do not always perform consistently when deadlines threaten. On different occasions, the efforts of Mary Ann Atkinson, Judy Jackson, and Eileen Minshull were necessary to keep the computers from going out the window.

FEDERAL BUDGET DEFICITS

INTRODUCTION

The economic news of the early 1980s has been dominated by talk of deficits in the U.S. federal government's budget. In part as a result of the significant tax cuts made in the early 1980s, in part as a result of the rapid growth in defense spending, in part as a result of the rapid growth in interest payments, and in part because other civilian spending was not cut very much, U.S. federal budget deficits changed from an average of 1.8 percent of gross national product (GNP) in the 1970s to more than 5 percent of GNP by fiscal year 1984. Projections done for the remainder of the decade had these deficits rising to close to 6 percent of GNP by 1990 unless rather stark and unprecedented measures were taken either to raise taxes or cut expenditures.

The gross numbers are even more impressive—or depressing. Beginning as a country with a very small federal budget, the U.S. government deficit was only $1 or $2 billion, even in the depth of the Great Depression. This deficit rose to a peak of $55 billion during World War II, but it dropped right down after the War, and, in fact, the federal budget was in surplus in all but one of the years between 1946 and 1952. Neither deficits nor surpluses were large throughout the 1950s and 1960s, even though the government was spending in excess of $30 billion a year on the Vietnam War during the late 1960s. The World War II record was not exceeded until the recession of 1975 when the budget deficit rose to $69 billion, but again, it dropped down and was only $16 billion as recently as 1979. Then the dam burst: The budget deficit rose to $148 billion in 1982, $179 billion in 1983, and it is projected to approach $300 billion in the next few years unless big changes are made.

A final way of looking at the numbers is in terms of the public debt. The deficit is what economists call a "flow"; that is, it is a difference between the flow of expenditures and the flow of receipts during a time period. Although it is legally possible for the government simply to print money to finance this deficit, in practice, almost all of the deficit is accounted for by having the federal government borrow from the private sector. This borrowing represents an increase in the cumulated "stock" of all such liabilities that have been built up in the past, called the *government* (or *national*, or *public*) *debt*. The gross interest-bearing public debt of the United States was $40 billion at the start and $235 billion (111 percent of GNP) at the end of World War II. The debt had risen to $715 billion by 1980, though because GNP had risen much more over this period, debt levels then dropped to just 27 percent of GNP. But now, this ratio has turned around: The stock of interest-bearing debt recently has passed over $1 trillion and is forecast to rise to close to $3 trillion by the end of the decade (without the big changes mentioned above); the ratio of debt to GNP could soon be back to about 50 percent of GNP.

The sheer amount of newsprint devoted to these large deficits during the past two years indicates that something must be going on—the deficits have dominated the economic portion of debates between presidential candidates; the deficits are alleged to have ruined the stock market; the deficits have led to a call for a Constitutional amendment; the American deficits have been the major topic of conversation at an economic summit meeting of the heads of all major trading countries; and the American deficits are said to be bankrupting the less-developed countries with large obligations to private banks. But for all of the opposition to deficits, the costs and benefits of these deficits are rarely stated and debated. Why are the deficits so bad? After all, people are working, the economy is growing, and technological progress is being made. How could the economy be performing that well if deficits are as terrible as everybody is saying? On the other side, if the deficits are that harmful, why does the United States—and just about all other countries—continue to run them?

In this book we try to answer these questions. We find that the particular large deficits under discussion—that is, those forecast for the balance of the decade—are harmful. But we do not believe that all deficits are harmful. We give our reasons for opposing some deficits and favoring others in a way that can be understood by noneconomists and that will also be helpful to beginning students of economics. Because by no means does everybody lose from the deficits, we also try to assess the pattern of gains and losses, both now and in the future. And we discuss what, if anything, can be done about the deficits—legislatively in the short run and constitutionally in the long run.

POLITICS

The book takes a nonpartisan view of deficits, without trying to attribute political responsibility for their occurrence. In any budget all items add to the total deficit, so it is never possible to isolate particular causes of deficits—they can occur because revenues fall or fail to rise, or because expenditures rise or fail to fall. When this mathematical proposition is introduced to a political setting, deficits can equally logically be attributed to the party that voted for big defense spending increases, the party that failed to cut social spending, or the party that passed large tax cuts. If political name-calling is the game, there is fertile ground for all comers, and it is not terribly productive to determine which ground is the more fertile.

We will try to sidestep political analyses in two other senses. Unlikely as it seems, it is possible that politicians at some point will get together and pass a series of measures that eliminate the deficits. In this case, many of the dire predictions made here and elsewhere become moot, at least temporarily. We are not going to speculate on the likelihood of such a sudden burst of fiscal responsibility, but we do point out that it does not destroy our motive in writing the book. The book is about what happens if the deficits *do* come to pass, not whether they *will* come to pass.

Finally, at the end of the book we propose some measures to deal with deficits, in both the short and long term. We do this with an eye mainly to the wisdom of the proposals from an economic standpoint, without regard to political feasibility. There are a number of reasons for such an approach. For one thing, notions of what measures are and what are not politically feasible can and do change very quickly, especially with the fear of large deficits hanging over the heads of politicians. We want to focus on the more permanent economic and social consequences of the measures. Moreover, we view our role as simply one of suggesting measures and evaluating their consequences, letting those involved in the political process determine which, if any, of these measures will pass.

THE PLAN OF THE BOOK

The specific plan of the book is as follows. Chapter 1 deals with a number of factual issues, describing what it means to have a deficit in the government's budget, according to different accounting conventions. Chapter 1 also addresses some conceptual issues, including what a budget deficit *should* try to measure, and it evaluates several ways in which budgetary information might be presented—the national income accounts (NIA) budget, a capital budget, and a weighted and unweighted high-employment budget. Chapter 1 also presents data on the different definitions of the deficit, to see if the present problem is merely one of accounting or is more basic. Without spoiling the story, we can give a quick summary of the chapter by saying that none of the new accounting concepts changes our view of the size of the upcoming deficits or their implications.

Chapter 2 is concerned with the macroeconomic impacts of budget deficits, however measured. We distinguish between short-run fiscal effects of deficits, which may often be desirable, and long-run effects, for which this evaluation is usually reversed. We also show how these analyses change in an "open" economy, where international capital flows are highly sensitive to interest rate differentials in various countries and where foreign exchange rates are flexible. This chapter is written for the noneconomist; we try to keep the analysis as simple as possible, but the plain truth is that macroeconomics can be confusing, and the chapter is much easier to follow, and much more enriching, if the reader has studied some macroeconomics in an introductory course. For those desiring to do some work on their own, the material in the appendices enables readers to explore things more deeply.

The chapter also talks about gainers and losers. A basic theme of the earlier chapters is that budget deficits can be viewed as an intergenerational transfer—payments for public services that are consumed now are pushed onto future generations, and this will lower the capital stock our children have to provide for their own living standards. Hence the general pattern of gainers and losers will be that old people living now will benefit from deficits, while the young and the unborn will lose. Moreover, there will be additional transfers among the present generation, as the rise in the interest rate or the value of the dollar will help certain industries and hurt others, help certain regions of the country and hurt others. The chapter discusses all of these issues, and provides a few illustrative estimates of their importance.

Chapter 3 covers what may become the ticking time bomb in the deficit question—the under-appreciated role of interest payments. When there is a deficit, interest rates will normally be forced up, hence raising interest payments automatically. Moreover, the stock of interest-bearing debt will also rise nearly automatically, providing for another upward push in interest payments. Some elementary algebra can then show how these two forces can, under quite reasonable assumptions, lead to a steadily growing share of the budget being used simply to pay the interest on the past debt. In this sense, deficits once incurred become increasingly difficult to eliminate, similar to the difficulty less-developed countries are confronting in paying off their debt to commercial banks these days. The problem is not yet nearly as serious with the U.S. federal budget, but it could easily become so. The chapter then gives a simple simulation of the hidden but dramatic role of interest payments in budgetary forecasts.

Chapter 4 talks about measures to correct the deficits on the spending side. Using the unassailable logic of focusing our efforts where the money is, we review and evaluate the promising ways that have been suggested for trimming the large and burgeoning expenditures—defense spending, social security and other pension payments, and government health insurance. The basic conclusion of this chapter is a pessimistic one: Barring fairly revolutionary changes, it is not likely to be possible to trim spending the requisite amount. Some adjustment will be necessary on the tax side. Chapter 5 then examines options on the tax side. It deals with efforts to broaden the base of the income tax, institute a national sales or value-added tax, and our own preferred notion of moving to a progressive expenditure tax, sometimes known as a lifetime income tax.

Chapter 6 takes a longer-term perspective on the deficit problem. Rather than appraising this spending measure or that tax, it deals with procedural measures such as the Budget Reform Act of 1974, proposals for giving the President line-item veto power, and constitutional limitations recently passed in several states. The pros and cons of these constitutional procedures are discussed, from both an economic and a legal standpoint.

Chapter 7 then provides a quick recapitulation to the book. We stress again the long-term harm we feel the deficits will do to the country's living standards, but also point out the difficulties, often underestimated, in making significant changes.

CHAPTER ONE
THE MEANING
AND SIGNIFICANCE
OF BUDGET DEFICITS

The general breast-beating about the budget deficits suggests that there is fairly widespread agreement both on how budget deficits should be measured and on their impact on the economy. In fact, neither is the case. Chapter 2 discusses the economic impact of budget deficits; in this chapter we stick to the prior, and easier, question of how budget deficits should be measured.

The proliferation of budgetary deficit measures is in large part due to confusion about what it is about budgets that should be measured. Politicans are used to thinking in terms of accounting concepts; bond traders are more concerned with credit flows; and business economists need a complete economy-wide income statement upon which to base their short-term outlook forecasts. We do not feel that any of these represents the most important aspect of fiscal policy. As we will argue throughout the book, we feel that the most important long-term aspect of fiscal policy is its impact on national capital formation. In this chapter we first show the connection between the deficit and capital formation. We then review some of the many measures that try to improve on the official deficit, showing how each can be rationalized as an attempt to better describe the capital formation impact of the deficit. We conclude by giving some actual budgetary data, historically and as it is projected into the future.

DEFICITS AND CAPITAL FORMATION

A convenient place to begin is with the national income accounts (NIA). All beginning macroeconomics students are taught that the total output of an economy in a year can be measured either by adding up all purchases in the economy, or by adding up all incomes earned from production. An illustration of this basic accounting convention is shown in Table 1.1. The top panel of the table adds up total output, or gross national product (GNP), on the expenditure side. United States GNP was $3310 billion in 1983, of which $2159 billion was sold to households in the form of consumption goods, $690 billion was sold to governments, $471 was sold to businesses for additions to the stock of productive capital (termed *capital investment* in the NIA), and a net of −$11 billion was sold to foreigners. It may appear surprising that the latter number is negative: The reason for this is that U.S. citizens bought from foreigners $11 billion more than was sold to foreigners in 1983. National production was therefore $11 billion less than the sum of national consumption, investment, and government purchases, and the $11 billion, net imports, must be deducted (or net exports added in) to measure production correctly.

To anticipate later use of these numbers, it is helpful to distinguish that production used to support current consumption from that used to support future consumption. Clearly, consumption spending supports today's consumption. The same can be said of government purchases, the overwhelming majority of which go to hire civil servants, soldiers, police, and school teachers, or to purchase office sup-

TABLE 1.1 U.S. Gross National Product in 1983: The Expenditure and Income Side

	BILLIONS CURRENT $[a]		
EXPENDITURE SIDE			
GNP	3310		
Consumption		2159	
Gross business investment		471	
Net exports		−11	
Government purchases		690	
INCOME USES SIDE			
GNP	3310		
Net taxes		565	
Indirect business taxes[b]			270
Corporate			76
Personal			406
Social insurance			272
Government transfers			−388
Government interest			−71
Business saving		473	
Depreciation allowances			377
Undistributed profits[c]			96
Household saving		113	
Consumption		2159	

[a] Details may not add to total because of rounding error.
[b] Net of subsidies of government enterprises.
[c] Corporate profits less dividends less corporate taxes plus a small adjustment for private interest payments.

Source: *The Economic Report of the President, February, 1984*, Tables B.1, B.19, B.20, B.21, and B.23.

plies and space for their use (more on this later). Just as clearly, investment, or capital formation, goes to build up the stock of machines and structures that can be used to produce future consumption goods The same can be said of net exports—were they positive, the nation would be accumulating foreign exchange that could be used to buy future imports. Hence we can think of private capial formation as the sum of gross investment and net exports.

The bottom panel of Table 1.1 shows how this income was used. Of the total income earned from production in 1983, a net of $565 billion was paid to governments in the form of what might be called "net taxes": The four types of taxes listed less two types of transfer payments that flowed in reverse, from governments to households. Business saving, in the form of depreciation allowances and profits after taxes and after dividends, was $473 billion. Households got the rest, and they used it either for consumption or for their own personal saving.

We can then see the connection between government deficits and capital formation by manipulating these numbers. Switching to some commonly used symbols, the equation for the top panel of the table is

$$Y = C + dK + G \tag{1}$$

where Y stands for GNP, C for consumption, G for government purchases, and dK for gross capital formation, the sum of all additions to the stock of productive equipment, structures, and foreign exchange balances. The equation for the bottom panel is

$$Y = T + Sb + Sh + C \tag{2}$$

where T stands for net taxes, Sb for business saving, and Sh for household saving.

Because the left side of both equations is Y, both right sides are equal to each other. Moreover, consumption, the common element on the right side, cancels out. Therefore, equating (1) and (2) and dropping consumption, we have

$$dK = T - G + Sb + Sh = Sg + Sp \tag{3}$$

Gross capital formation is equal to net taxes less government purchases (T − G), here called Sg, plus the private saving done by businesses and households (Sb + Sh), here called Sp. As is routinely done in elementary macroeconomics, we have established that gross investment equals gross saving. But for our purposes it is important also to show that we can disaggregate gross saving into its governmental (Sg) and its private (Sp) components.

Note that the concept of government saving in the above expression is exactly the government surplus, or the negative of the government deficit. This then tips us off to the reason that deficits are, or may be, so important. A deficit shows up in (3) as a negative value for Sg, one that, other things equal, may lower national capital formation. Putting it another way, a deficit can be thought of as governmental dissaving, normally offsetting some of the private saving that would otherwise be devoted to capital formation.

DIFFERENT MEASURES
OF BUDGET DEFICITS

The preceding connection between government budget deficits and national capital formation was based on nothing more than elementary national income accounting relationships. But although these relationships are indicative, they are also very simple. Simple measures can oversimplify, and attempts to revise and refine budgetary definitions are necessary if we are to state better the connection between deficits and capital formation.

A first adjustment refers to what are known as *asset transactions*. The budget deficit in the capital formation identity (3) is based on an equation that adds up all the income earned from production in the economy. The official budget deficit, shown in Table 1.2, includes some items that change private incomes—transfer payments, purchases, and taxes—and some that do not. For example, when the post office buys land to put up a new building, nobody has gained income or wealth—the previous owner merely exchanged the land for money—and no new productive

TABLE 1.2   The U.S. Federal Budget Deficit in Fiscal Years 1979 and 1983

	BILLIONS CURRENT $^{a}		
	1979	1983	CHANGE
Official budget deficit	28	195	167
Net asset purchases[b]	(−13)	(−9)	
NIA budget deficit	15	186	171
Real interest correction[c]	(−22)	(−45)	
Corrected interest budget deficit	−7	141	148
Federal capital formation[d]	(−24)	(−38)	
Capital budget deficit	−31	103	134
Cyclical correction[e]	(21)	(−49)	
Structural capital budget deficit	−10	54	64

[a] Details may not add to totals because of rounding error.
[b] Includes also some timing adjustments and capital transactions in connection with off-shore oil leases.
[c] Assuming the real interest rate was 3 percent in 1979 (when the nominal rate on federal debt was 6.3 percent) and 4 percent in 1983 (when the nominal rate was 8 percent).
[d] Nondefense construction and equipment purchases plus one-half of defense construction and equipment, as explained in the text.
[e] Based on what is called the middle expansion trend GNP, from Frank de Leeuw and Thomas M. Holloway, "Cyclical Adjustment of the Federal Budget and Federal Debt," *Survey of Current Business*, December, 1983, Table 3.
Source: *The Economic Report of the President, February, 1984*, Tables B.73, B.74, and B.76; *Survey of Current Business,* July, 1983, and successive issues, Table 3.7B; de Leeuw and Holloway, "Cyclical Adjustment"; *Budget of the U.S. Government, Fiscal Year, 1985,* Special Analysis D, Table D-2.

capital was created—the land existed already. Because these asset sales are not included in GNP, which tries to measure new production, asset sales must be excluded from government purchases as well to generate a deficit that is consistent with the rest of the national income accounts. To think about this another way, asset sales should be excluded because, in not reflecting an addition to net government liabilities, spending to purchase existing assets is not governmental dissaving and it should not be included in the budget deficit. Once these asset exchanges items are excluded, as shown in Table 1.2, we can generate what is referred to as the *NIA budget deficit*, so labeled because it is consistent with all other items in the national accounts.

A similar type of adjustment has been required by the recent experience of the American economy with inflation. Inflation makes lenders worse off because their assets are repaid in depreciated dollars; borrowers are better off for the same reason. Once inflation is anticipated, lenders build an inflation premium into interest rates simply to protect themselves from erosion in asset values. As an example, if lenders and borrowers could agree on a 3-percent interest rate when neither expected inflation, they would be expected to settle at 8 percent if both anticipated a 5-percent inflation. The lender would receive what is called the *nominal interest rate* of 8 percent, 5 percent of which would compensate for inflation, and still get the same 3-percent real return, called the *real interest rate*. The borrower would in effect pay the 3-percent real interest rate through a similar calculation.

All of this happens with federal government debt, too. Inflation helps the debtor—in this case, the federal government—and hurts all lenders. Consequently, lenders drive up the rate the federal government must pay when it borrows during inflationary periods. As this happens, nominal interest payments rise, even though the same real payment is being made from the federal government to its creditors. To measure correctly the income gain of the private sector and loss to the government, only the real interest payments should be counted as an expenditure; the remaining payments simply compensate the lenders for reductions in the real value of their debt stemming from inflation. Two economists, Robert Eisner and Paul Pieper, have pointed this out, and have computed a new set of accounts that includes only real interest payments as expenditures. We call this Eisner–Pieper deficit the corrected-interest budget deficit.[1] Table 1.2 makes a very simple interest correction, and as can be seen there, this correction does lower interest payments and the budget deficit by $22 and $45 billion in the two years.

A third adjustment involves direct capital formation by the government. Per equation (1), spending on final output is divided up into government purchases and capital formation, with all of the government's purchases considered as consumption. Clearly the vast majority of purchases by the federal government are for consumption-like services, but not all. Some government spending is for capital purchases such as roads, bridges, or guided missiles.

It is often argued that federal budgetary accounts should be kept in the form of a capital budget, under which only consumption purchases would be included in G and the deficit, whereas capital purchases would be considered as a part of gross national investment. In fact, it is now possible to compute such a capital budget deficit for the federal government, on the basis of information given in Special Analysis D of the annual budget document. Three types of investment-like spending are listed there:

1. Equipment and structures for national defense, totaling $60 billion in fiscal 1983
2. Equipment and structures for nondefense, mainly water projects, totaling $8 billion in fiscal 1983
3. Grants to state governments for their capital purchases, totaling $21 billion in fiscal 1983.

Referring to the third entry in the list, grants to state governments have been found to stimulate very little capital spending by state governments. These governments seem to use federal capital grant money to finance capital construction projects (for roads, schools, hospitals, and sewage treatment plants) they would have done anyway, in effect using the grant money to finance current expenditures or tax reduction.[2] If such is the case, federal capital grants are not really used to finance capital construction and they should not be considered as capital purchases in a federal capital budget.

The question of how to count defense purchases of hardware is more complicated. A small share is for construction expenditures for military housing and nuclear power plants, clearly capital formation. But 90 percent of the total is for military hardware such as planes, ships, and missiles. Although this hardware looks like physical investment, it has a very high rate of technological obsolescence, which means that it does not provide defense "services" for very long. Moreover, some of it is undoubtedly waste, either in the excess cost sense or in the sense that certain missiles may cause the Soviet bloc to spend more on their own missiles, and actually lower defense services (these issues are discussed in more detail in Chapter 4). The gross amount of $60 billion listed in Special Analysis D makes no adjustment for either factor, and thus potentially overstates the true investment component of defense hardware purchases. On the other hand, we later argue that even the noninvestment component of defense spending could in some sense be considered as investment in the future security of the country.

With all of these big issues at stake, it is obviously impossible to come close to a true capital budget in the economist's sense of the term. Using a more modified physiocratic standard (capital investment is only in goods that look like capital), with an assumed high rate of technological obsolescence for defense, we have made a rough estimate of true federal capital purchases by considering none of the capital grants as investment, all of nondefense construction as investment, and half of defense equipment purchases as investment. Under these assumptions, federal capital purchases are $24 and $38 billion, respectively, in the two years, and the new capital budget deficit is cut to $103 billion for 1983, with a surplus (negative deficit) or $31 billion for 1979.[3]

A fourth change involves the business cycle. Referring to (3), private investment changes with economic activity, rising in boom periods as firms try to get more capital to produce more output, and falling in recessions. The government deficit changes automatically as tax revenues rise in booms and fall in recessions, and as unemployment insurance transfers behave in exactly the reverse direction. Private saving also rises and falls because profits rise in booms and fall in recessions, as does household saving. When all of the items in (3) have such a strong cyclical component, it becomes rather difficult to make comparisons of deficits over time because of the cycle. To take one famous example, in the Great Depression the Roosevelt Administration kept trying to eliminate budget deficits by raising taxes and cutting purchases, but every time that happened, the reduced buying power would start a new downturn, and new deficits were generated. Historians examining Roosevelt's budget policies have been thoroughly misled as to their true nature, considering them much more expansionary than was in fact the case.

To correct for this cyclical variability, economists beginning with Cary Brown have computed what was formerly known as a full-employment budget surplus (or deficit), and is now known as a structural budget surplus.[4] To make this computation, analysts simply assume that income is at some standardized normal- or high-employment level, and then measure normal tax revenues and transfer payments. The new name for the budget surplus makes no difference at all—all calculations are done just as in the early days when the surplus was called a full-employment surplus—and the unemployment rate used to make the standardized comparison matters very little. What does matter is that the budget deficit or surplus be computed on a standardized basis, as is done in Table 1.2. The differing adjustments shown indicate that the economy was in a position of greater-than-normal employment levels of output in 1979, implying that the actual surplus of $31 billion exceeded the structural surplus of $10 billion. In 1983, on the other hand, the economy was in a position of less-than-normal levels of output and the actual deficit of $103 billion exceeded the structural deficit of $54 billion.

Until now the adjustments have been in the direction of stating more correctly the relevant income or capital formation change implied by the budget deficit. But there have also been some proposals to correct for the fact that not all items in the budget have the same dollar-for-dollar impact on private investment. To take one example, suppose that households devote $0.75 of every dollar's change in their income to private consumption, while businesses retain the entire dollar in undistributed profits. A dollar personal tax cut with no change in expenditures will lower Sg in equation (3) by one dollar and raise Sh by $0.25, for a net drop in economy-wide saving of $0.75. In the short run, such a change will raise income, but through a process explained in the next chapter, in the long run income should be roughly constant and capital formation will be forced to drop $0.75. A dollar business tax cut will, on the other hand, simply be transferred to corporate profits; it will not raise income at all, and it will have no long-run effect on capital formation: Sb will rise by exactly the drop in Sg. This simple example shows how the composition of the deficit between types of taxes, and taxes and expenditures, does matter. Several economists have shown how these compositional problems could be eliminated by weighting budgetary totals and computing an adjusted high-employment budget deficit or surplus.[5]

The preceding example brings out two points that are incessantly debated by macroeconomists these days. Both involve the fact that the right side of (3) contains two elements—government saving and private saving. One source of confusion surrounding the equation involves the proper definition of a saving stimulus. It is commonly argued that taxes on households should be cut to encourage private saving. Such an argument is certainly misleading and almost certainly wrong. If taxes are cut by one dollar, the immediate impact is for Sg to fall by one dollar. Then private saving has to rise by *more* than one dollar for aggregate saving to rise. Simply arguing that private saving will rise is not sufficient—private saving must rise by a large enough amount to offset the drop in government saving (that is, the higher deficit).

The second source of confusion surrounding equation (3) goes back to a point initially made (and dismissed) by the nineteenth-century economist David Ricardo, and recently revived by Robert Barro.[6] The Barro argument is that if households are informed about fiscal policy, have long time horizons, and perhaps plan their own spending in light of the economic welfare of their offspring, changes in the budget deficit could have very little effect on economic activity. A rise in the deficit, for example, could lead to the view that taxes will have to go up eventually, and to the related view that private households should save more to prepare for these eventual tax liabilities, either in their lives or the lives of their offspring (or *their* offspring). Hence the initial drop in Sg could be completely offset by a rise in Sh, with fiscal changes thus having very little impact on the economy. If Barro is right about this, many of the dire predictions about the budget deficit are overdrawn. Any long-term predictions would be exactly the same if there were a budget surplus, or no change in the budgetary position.

A final way of adjusting budget deficits was suggested by Laurence Kotlikoff.[7] Kotlikoff reasons that the point of accumulating capital is to provide for consumption possibilities for the future, and that many actions that do change consumption possibilities for the present and future generations alike are not even recorded in conventional budgets. If, for example, Congress were to legislate rises in social security benefits for present-day workers without corresponding tax increases, the present generation will enjoy increased consumption opportunities, with future generations paying the cost. Because these present workers are not yet Social Security recipients, such a change will not raise the deficit at all in the short run, but it will act much like a deficit in transferring consumption opportunities from the future to the present. Kotlikoff's solution is to provide, perhaps as a supplement to the budget, a statement of how governmental policy is affecting households of every age, and thereby completely adjust for the impact of the budget and non-budget items alike on the entire set of future consumption possibilities. It would take a number of strong, and arbitrary, assumptions to do this systematically for all budget changes, and one could imagine the fun the press would have with the idea. But one could certainly retain the spirit of the suggestion by looking at the impact of fiscal changes on households of different ages. That is exactly what we try to do in our discussions of the impact of present-day deficits in later chapters.

ACTUAL BUDGET DEFICITS

The numbers shown in Table 1.2 indicate at least some of the adjustments in budget deficits that provide for a better statement of their impact on aggregate capital formation. It is apparent from reading down the table that most of these adjustments work in the direction of lowering the true budget deficits. Some of the officially reported transactions simply represent purchases of assets from the private sector, and do not add to government's net liabilities. Some of the interest expenses are simply compensating lenders for anticipated inflation, and are not adding to real government liabilities. Some expenditures are to purchase government-owned capital, and should not count as a reduction in total capital formation. Much of the 1983 deficit was caused by the fact that the economy had not yet recovered from the deep recession of 1982, and this part should be eliminated before year-to-year comparisons are made. When all these changes are made, the official budget deficit of $195 billion for 1983, the largest recorded in American history, is reduced by more than 70 percent to $54 billion, and looks a good bit less alarming. But lest these adjustments lead to a sense of complacency, there are still three things to worry about.

For one thing, even after all the adjustments, the budget deficit has grown by $64 billion, almost 2 percent of GNP, since 1979. In historical terms, this is already a very sharp change—except during World War II, the budget deficit corrected for these various factors has never grown so abruptly. This change was almost entirely due to increases in consumption-like purchases of the government (remember, we have eliminated the capital purchases) and to cuts in personal taxes, which mainly stimulate private consumption. Hence even this smaller deficit can be expected to cause a drop in the rate of national capital formation of $64 billion, about 14 percent of the gross capital formation of Table 1.1.

A second problem involves the future outlook. In Fig. 1.1 we show the simple NIA budget deficit as a share of GNP, in the past and using reasonable projections for the future. While there are cyclical oscillations in the series, it is clear that U.S. budget deficits are not only not coming down, but they will get larger unless significant future changes are made. The main reason is the steady growth of interest payments. This process will be described more carefully in Chapter 3, but for now it can be seen that if the $64 billion growth in the deficit generates that amount of new debt, the average interest rate on which is now about 9 percent, government spending and the deficit must rise by $6 billion ever afterward. In this regard, the recent sharp upturn in the ratio of the interest-bearing debt to GNP is a very ominous development.

The third problem involves very directly the reason we worry about deficits to begin with. We saw above that these deficits are likely to lead to a drop in national capital formation. This could not happen at a worse time for the American economy. Figure 1.2 reports on the share of output devoted to capital formation for the United States and the six other important developed economies with which the U.S. economy is most often compared. Figure 1.2 shows that our national capital formation rate is below all of the countries except West Germany, and not

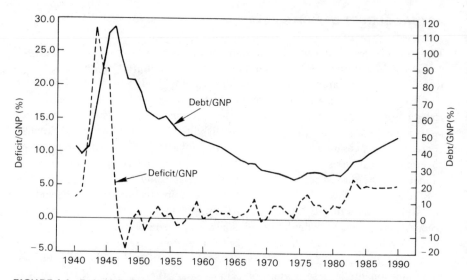

FIGURE 1.1 Federal Deficits and Debt as a Percent of GNP, 1940-1990, Actual Numbers 1940-1984. Congressional Budget Office Projections 1985-1990.

Source: *The Economic Report of the President, February, 1984,* Tables B.1 and B.73; Congressional Budget Office, *The Economic and Budget Outlook: Fiscal Years 1986-1990,* February, 1985, Table II-1.

even close to that of Japan. And these shares were measured up to 1981, when U.S. budget deficits were almost exactly equal to that of the average for all other six countries. After 1981, U.S. deficits began rising sharply, and it is reasonable to expect the share of U.S. output devoted to capital formation to fall even further behind those of the other countries.

If this evidence were not sufficient to establish the case that *reductions* in national capital formation are not desirable right now, there are two other persuasive pieces of evidence. First is the fact that United States rises in productivity have slackened way off recently—output per worker grew by 2.1 percent per year during the 1960s, but by only 0.4 percent per year in the 1970s and early 1980s. Continuation of these trends will limit the basic economic growth that has probably generated the innate sense of optimism and future orientation normally demonstrated by American businesses and households. Second is the fact, to be stressed below, that with the opening of national borders to greater trade and capital flows, the United States will have to compete very vigorously in world markets in the future. There is no worse way to do that than to cut back drastically on capital formation.

Hence even though the various adjustments to the budget deficit may put the true budget problem in a clearer light, there are absolutely no grounds for neglect of the problem. Even the smaller adjusted deficit has grown quite sharply in recent years; it seems likely to grow even more in the near future as the interest burden accumulates; and these events take place in an economy that is already saving little

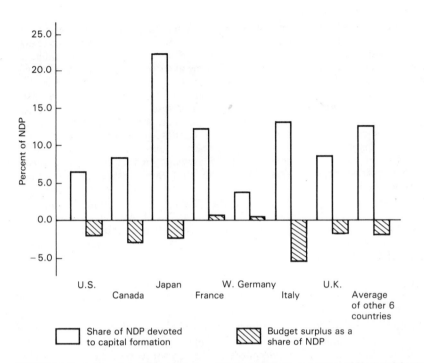

FIGURE 1.2 International Comparisons of Budget Deficits and Rates of National Capital Formation, 1976–1981 (as a percent of net domestic product).

Source: OECD, Department of Economics and Statistics, *National Accounts, 1976–1981,* vol. 2.

compared to our neighbors. It is definitely the wrong time for the country to run large deficits.

NOTES

[1] Robert Eisner and Paul J. Pieper, "A New View of the Federal Debt and Budget Deficits," *American Economic Review,* vol. 74, March, 1984, pp. 11–29. Eisner and Pieper adjust government debt for two factors—the change in its real value in inflations, and another change in real value when real interest rates change. Our adjustment excludes the latter phenomenon. To make our correction, we assumed that the average inflation rate for the past three years was an inflation forecast for the present year, and then used this assumption to measure the difference between nominal and real interest rates on the federal debt.

[2] See Edward M. Gramlich, "An Econometric Analysis of the New Federalism," *Brookings Papers on Economic Activity,* 2:1982, for an empirical analysis that arrives at just this conclusion. Other articles arriving at similar conclusions are cited there.

[3] A recent article by Robert Heilbroner in *The New Yorker,* July 30, 1984, entitled "Reflections: The Deficit," tried to deemphasize the gravity of the up-

coming deficits, largely based on a statistic that federal capital spending was $180 billion, much larger than the number we use here. Part of the difference was Heilbroner's surprising (for a liberal) acceptance of *all* of the defense capital spending as capital investment. Part was his inclusion of some asset transaction items that have already been excluded from the NIA deficit. Part was his acceptance of capital grants as investment, a treatment we quarrel with on empirical grounds. And part of the difference was his inclusion of $65 billion of research and development expenditures, the vast majority for defense or grants, as investment. The latter may be investment in some sense, but it is not treated as capital formation in the rest of the national accounts or by other countries and their accounts. It would then distort both times series comparisons of the United States and cross-country comparisons to consider defense research expenditures in the United States as investment expenditures.

[4] E. Cary Brown, "Fiscal Policy in the Thirties: A Reappraisal," *American Economic Review*, vol. 46, December, 1956, pp. 857–879. Although the renaming of the concept has nowhere been explicitly discussed, it is undoubtedly related to growing pessimism about the ability of the economy to attain levels of full employment with stable prices.

[5] An early attempt to do this was again by Brown, "Fiscal Policy." A more complete effort was made by Edward M. Gramlich, "The Behavior and Adequacy of the United States Federal Budget," *Yale Economic Essays*, vol. 6, Spring, 1966, pp. 98–159.

[6] Robert J. Barro, "Are Government Bonds Net Wealth?" *Journal of Political* argument seems extreme, it is in some sense only a generalization of what economists call the permanent income hypothesis: The hypothesis that consumers plan consumption spending over their life cycle and try to forecast changes in taxes and expenditures. The inventors of this hypothesis are Milton Friedman, *A Theory of the Consumption Function*, Princeton University Press, 1957; and Franco Modigliani and Richard Brumberg, "Utility Analysis and the Consumption Function: An Interpretation of Cross Section Data," in Kenneth Kurihara (ed.) *Post Keynesian Economics*, Rutgers University Press, 1954, pp. 388–436.

[7] Laurence J. Kotlikoff, "Taxation and Saving—A Neoclassical Perspective," *Journal of Economic Literature*, vol. 22, December, 1984, pp. 1576–1629.

CHAPTER TWO
MACROECONOMICS

The Keynesian revolution, beginning in the Great Depression, firmly established one important postulate of economic policy making: That changes in the government's budget, called *fiscal policy*, can be used to further macroeconomic goals. The particular macroeconomic goals can differ. In the short run, the dominant concern is generally to stabilize aggregate demand around its desired high employment level, trying to prevent recessions on one side and demand pull inflation on the other. In the long run, the dominant concern is, as we have seen, to provide for a reasonable amount of saving and capital formation throughout the economy. The fiscal prescriptions to achieve these differing goals also will often differ. But though there is inevitable controversy about which goals ought to be pursued in what way by what fiscal changes, there is broad agreement that deficits, representing in some sense a summary measure of fiscal policy, should be evaluated in terms of their impact on various macroeconomic goals.

In this chapter we try to explain these ideas. We first review macroeconomics in the short run, and describe how fiscal policy should be set in response to various outside forces. We then do the same for macroeconomics in the long run. We proceed to complicate the explanations by considering what happens when economies are open to international trade and capital flows and when foreign exchange rates are flexible, a set of conditions that seems to describe the policy-making environment for the United States at present. We then use these general lessons to evaluate, from a macroeconomic standpoint, today's large deficits and tomorrow's anticipated larger deficits. We conclude by trying to show the pattern of economic gains and losses resulting from the deficits, within the present generation and over time for different generations.

SHORT-TERM STABILIZATION

The reason for distinguishing between short- and long-term macroeconomics is that in the short run some important variables cannot reasonably be changed. One such variable is the level of the capital stock—the sum total of machinery, equipment and structures used to produce the economy's output. At present in the United States this stock is so large that one year's new capital investment amounts to only about 3 percent of the stock. Hence even if there were enormous changes in investment in new capital, say, capital formation were suspended altogether, there would still be only minor changes in the total stock. For all intents and purposes, we can think of the capital stock as fixed over one year's time.

Two other variables that can be considered as relatively fixed over one year's time—or at least as moving independently of the year's demand and supply conditions—are the levels of prices and wages. This statement may seem surprising from both a theoretical and a factual standpoint. From a theoretical standpoint, it would appear that firms could change their prices and/or wages any time they wanted and that these variables should not be considered as independent of demand and supply. The only problem is that much evidence is building up that, at least in the short run, firms simply do not behave that way. Many firms do most of their business with steady customers, and develop long-term pricing arrangements with these customers that preclude sharp changes in prices every time demand or supply conditions change. Many workers spend their entire career working for the same firm, and rather than changing with the ups and downs of labor market conditions, their wage behaves more like an installment payment on a lifetime of wages. This sluggishness of wages is most vividly illustrated in the case of union contracts, which actually do fix wages for periods of up to three years, but most of the rest of us not on union contracts have wages that are just as independent of short-term changes in demand and supply.[1]

It also seems surprising to talk about relatively fixed prices and wages from a factual standpoint. After all, inflation is nothing more than the growth in wages and prices over time, and it should be perfectly obvious that inflation exists, sometimes to a seemingly dangerous degree. But it is important to recognize that although prices and wages do indeed change over time, they change at relatively predetermined rates, more or less independent of demand and supply in a particular year. For example, in two recent years, 1975 and 1982, the economy suffered quite serious recessions, with unemployment rates exceeding any known since the Great Depression of the 1930s. Even though the standard microeconomic lesson would be that prices and wages should fall in periods of such excess supply, in fact both prices and wages rose. The reason was that so much inflationary momentum was built into the system from previous inflations that even the large recessions made only slight dents in these inflations.[2]

It is this sluggishness of prices and wages that leads to the short-term stabilization problem. If prices and wages were perfectly flexible in the short run, they would rise when demand exceeded supply, and fall when it fell short of supply. When demand is high, potential spenders would be encouraged to wait and potential producers would be encouraged to supply, hence eliminating the excess demand.[3] The reverse would happen when demand was deficient. There would be little need for the government to try to stabilize aggregate spending in such a situation. But if prices and wages respond very sluggishly to movements in demand and supply, the economy is not so lucky. Then there will be periods of excess demand and supply. Output and employment will rise when there is excess demand and fall when there is excess supply. Movements on either side are costly—demand pull inflation is generated by the booms, and people are out of work in the recessions. A case can be built for having the government, through its budget, try to smooth out the damaging cycles.

The way in which this can be done is illustrated in Fig. 2.1, which graphs the basic saving-investment identity developed in the previous chapter. In this chart investment, called dK (for the change in the capital stock), is assumed to be completely independent of GNP (Y). One could introduce some dependence, but the basic analytical story would be the same. Saving, the sum of private and government saving, is assumed to be positively related to GNP. Both corporate profits and household saving, the two major components of private saving, rise when GNP rises. Moreover, as we saw in the last chapter, the government surplus (Sg) also rises when GNP rises. To make things simple, we will assume the economy starts in a position where the budget is balanced (Sg = 0), and investment and private saving are equal at the desired high employment level of output (Y*).

Now assume some outside event causes a reduction in investment and shifts the dK line down to dK'. If nothing were done, GNP would drop to Y_1, implying unemployment of all the labor now not needed to produce the lower level of output. As said above, if prices and wages were to drop quickly, the unemployment would not occur. But when prices are sluggish, the only way output can be kept near its desired high employment level is for the saving function also to shift down

FIGURE 2.1 Saving-Investment Equilibrium.

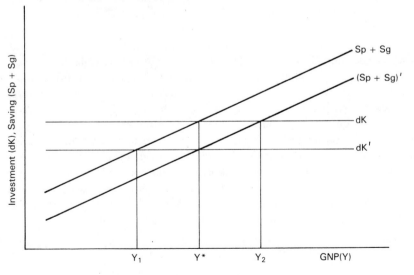

to $(Sp + Sg)'$. The easiest way to bring this about is to have the government run a deficit (with $Sg < 0$). In this case the government would either raise expenditures or cut taxes to keep Y close to Y*. Indeed, if investment depends positively on the level of GNP, deficits under the above circumstances may even *increase* investment by keeping it higher than it otherwise would have been in the recession.

[The above reasoning summarizes the basic case for deficits. If investment has declined anyway, if prices and wages are so sluggish that there will be large swings in output and employment, and if government policy can be well adapted to the cyclical declines, deficits can prove a valuable way to stabilize incomes, output, and employment. The reasoning is the essence of the Keynesian revolution in macroeconomics, the teachings of which have preoccupied macroeconomists ever since Keynes' famous book was written in the mid-1930s. Although we make no attack on the reasoning, it should be pointed out (and often is not) that when any of these conditions does not hold, the case cannot be made, or at least cannot be made as emphatically.]

[Even at this level, there is one cost to expansionary fiscal policy not brought out in the simple analysis, a phenomenon termed the "crowding out" of investment. For those with sufficient interest and/or training, we explain crowding out graphically in Appendix A, here only recounting the process verbally. As the drop in investment lowers income, the demand for money used to finance all transactions in the economy also drops. If the supply of money is kept fixed by the Federal Reserve, and recently that is the way the "Fed" has operated, the price of money, or the interest rate, will also drop. This drop in interest rates encourages firms to invest more, and partially offsets the initial drop in investment. To the extent that deficits prevent the drop in income *and* interest rates, they can be said to "crowd out" some investment, even in this case where they are stabilizing what would otherwise be a damaging recession.]

But it is possible to go beyond this and describe instances where deficit spending could have much more serious costs, even in the short run. Suppose the dK line did not shift down initially, but the government ran a deficit anyway. Then in the short run output would rise to Y_2. As before, this rise in Y would raise interest rates and crowd out some investment, hence lowering both capital formation and GNP. In addition, although the high level of output can be sustained temporarily, in the long run it cannot. Attempts to produce at greater than full employment levels of output will eventually lead to scarcities, bottlenecks, and other causes of what is known as *demand pull inflation*. Hence prices will rise more than would otherwise be the case, causing a reduction in the effective real supply of money and driving up interest rates even more (see Appendix A for more details). Eventually, the rise in interest rates will completely crowd out investment and force the dK line down to dK', making the equilibrium output again Y*, but with a lower level of investment. In this case the deficit spending causes an inflationary boom and some drop in investment in the short run and a further drop in investment in the long run, neither of which can be considered desirable outcomes.

Therefore, as far as stabilization policy goes, the wisdom or lack of wisdom of deficits depends on the cyclical needs of the day. If investment is dropping, prices are sticky, and crowding out is modest, deficit spending can boost output and prevent costly unemployment with a minimal loss of resources devoted to capital formation and a minimal drop in future living standards. If investment is rising, demand pull inflation is threatening, and crowding effects are strong, deficits can be inflationary and reduce the resources devoted to capital formation.

LONG-TERM CAPITAL FORMATION

We have distinguished the short from the long run by calling the short run that horizon over which some important variables were fixed, or independent of demand and supply movements. In the long run, everything has a chance to change and very little can be considered fixed. The stock of capital that was fixed in the short run because one year's investment is small relative to the entire cumulated stock is no longer fixed—there are now many years' investment that can change, and that will alter the stock. Prices and wages that move sluggishly in the short run because of quasi-contractual arrangements now also have a chance to respond to demand and supply movements as these arrangements are renegotiated.

A good example of the difference this assumption can make is in the second example discussed above. If deficit spending pulls Y above Y* for some period of time, eventually prices and wages will rise more rapidly than would otherwise be the case, and cause the dK schedule and Y to fall back down. In like fashion, the long-term flexibility of prices and wages assures that over this horizon prices and wages operate so as to eventually keep Y equal to Y*.

To work through this long-term example, suppose that an expansionary budget deficit (Sg < 0) is not offset by a Barro-like rise in private saving (Sp is constant). If the total saving schedule is held down in this way, the dK line eventually shifts to equate saving and investment at the normal high employment output level Y*. Deficit spending that takes Y above Y* thus causes higher interest rates, a crowding out of some investment, and a downward shift of the dK schedule; government surpluses cause less inflation than would otherwise be the case, lower interest rates, more investment, and a higher dK line. In effect, the investment line adjusts to the net shift in the saving line, and in determining the long-run impact of deficits, we can simply ignore investment and focus on what happens to the aggregate saving schedule as a result of fiscal changes. To the extent that Barro's view holds, of course, the next shift in the saving line is smaller because changes in government fiscal policy are offset by changes in private saving.

Another important long-term proposition is that there will be competition among potential investors in capital equipment, and that this competition will drive the marginal return to capital investment down to equality with the real (inflation-corrected) interest rate. Suppose the marginal return were above the interest rate.

Then firms could raise profits by investing more. They could borrow at the real interest rate and gain the marginal return on capital investment. This would lead them to expand the capital stock until the gap no longer existed. In equilibrium the marginal return to capital investment, sometimes called the *marginal product of capital*, should be approximately equal to the real interest rate.

Appendix B describes an analytical apparatus that uses all of these assumptions, called a *neoclassical growth model*. The assumptions in a growth model are almost diametrically opposed to those used in analyzing short-run movements in the economy. In short-term analysis the sluggishness of prices and wages allows us to treat aggregate output, Y, as a variable; in long-term analysis the variability of prices and wages forces us to assume the continued existence of high employment levels of output and to take Y as dependent only on the stock of capital and labor. In short-term analysis the capital stock is fixed; in long-term analysis it is not. In short-term analysis output is determined by the equilibration of investment and saving; in long-term analysis investment adjusts to saving.

The point of the growth model analysis given in Appendix B is to show how changes in the economy's saving rate, such as those caused by persistent government deficits or surpluses not offset by private saving, ultimately work themselves out in changes in an economy's capital–labor ratio and living standards. If the firms, households, and governments in an economy choose to devote a higher share of their annual output to capital formation, the amount of capital each worker has to work with will eventually rise, as will output per worker and, under certain conditions (which are fulfilled in the United States), consumption per worker. Saving more ultimately leads to higher living standards—present-day consumption is sacrificed for the sake of future consumption.

This is what is ultimately disturbing about the government deficits. As discussed in the previous chapter, the United States already saves less than other countries with similar economies. Government deficits not reflecting added government capital formation and not offset by private saving increases imply a reduction in the amount of saving. Ultimately this will lower the economy's capital–labor ratio and living standards. It is as if the economy is on a consumption binge.

THE OPEN ECONOMY

The preceding analyses, in both the short and long runs, have dealt with what has come to be known as the *closed economy case*—there was assumed to be no foreign trade and no importing or exporting of capital from abroad. In the real world, there are significant capital flows, and exchange rates are flexible. These two assumptions can change the lessons for fiscal policy quite dramatically.

Take first the short-run stabilization problem. We have pointed out that when the government ran deficits, they would drive up interest rates and crowd out some investment. In open economies, the crowding-out problem takes on much more significance, because now the rise in interest rates attracts capital from abroad, as foreigners try to gain the higher return on their capital. This capital inflow raises demand for dollars and their value, which in turn means that U.S. exports are more expensive in foreign countries and foreign imports are cheaper in this country. Sales of exports are likely to decline and sales of imports to rise, implying that net exports, the difference between exports and imports, drop as the deficits raise interest rates. Instead of crowding out only investment, deficits crowd out net exports as well. Because net exports are an important component of total production, deficits are not as likely to provide the impetus to bring an economy out of a recession when the economy is open. Whatever case could be made for fiscal policy to stabilize output in a closed economy, the case becomes weaker in an open economy with flexible exchange rates.[4]

The same is true in the long run. In the long run it is likely that international capital flows will bring domestic interest rates into equality with foreign rates, and provide a ready outlet for all domestic saving at the world rate of interest. In a closed economy, if the United States persistently saves very little, the capital-labor ratio would be low and the marginal product of capital high. If the United States saves a lot, the capital–labor ratio would be high and the marginal product of capital low. In an open economy, the marginal product of capital and the amount of capital located in the country are both set by the world interest rate. United States saving rates do not affect either the amount or the productivity of capital; they only determine how much of the worldwide stock is owned by U.S. residents. The less the United States saves, the less capital it owns, and the less U.S. citizens realize the returns on capital as income. In a closed economy, one of the limits to high saving is the fact that as capital becomes plentiful, its marginal return declines. In an open economy, this limit is removed because U.S. savers can always find a profitable foreign outlet for their saving. The open economy circumstances would again seem to place a higher value on saving and new wealth accumulation, and to raise the costs of persistent deficits.

And it is easy to make the case against U.S. deficits even stronger. We should remember that the country now attracting capital in this world economy is one of the richer economies, the United States, whereas the countries giving up the capital are often still-developing countries. Even if the world interest rate remains fixed, a standard assumption in open economy models, for the United States to attract capital from worldwide savings pools seems a misallocation. But if the U.S. deficits should attract enough capital to pull up worldwide interest rates, then the United States is enjoying its consumption binge at the expense of future generations in countries that are much poorer. There is, in effect, a crowding out of world investment.

THE CURRENT SITUATION

These general remarks can now be used to give an evaluation of present-day government deficits— are they desirable or undesirable? Referring back to Fig. 1.1, it can be seen that in 1982, when the economy was in recession and the unemployment rate attained damaging high levels, the actual NIA budget deficit was 3.6 percent of

GNP. In 1983, when the economy was growing rapidly, the deficit rose to 6 percent of GNP. For the balance of the decade, unemployment rates are projected to be even lower than in 1983, but deficit ratios are projected to be nearly as high. The pattern is all wrong.

The problem is not simply that deficits exist. An evaluation based on our above analysis is more complicated. Although there was surely some crowding out both of new investment and net exports, it appears that 1982 fiscal policy was more or less appropriate. The economy was suffering, and the deficits almost certainly were one helpful factor in supporting its recovery. Essentially the same was true in 1975, 1961, and in other postwar years when there were large recessions. Based on this evidence, it seems mistaken to abandon all fiscal efforts to stabilize GNP, as some commentators want to do. Fiscal policy, in the form of occasional large budget deficits, still can play, and has played, a useful role in limiting business cycles.

Having said that, there seems little doubt that for the present and future, deficits are and will be much too high. In the short run the superimposition of an extremely expansionary fiscal policy on a very vigorous economic recovery risks a renewed outbreak of inflation (because Y will be pushed above Y*), something that almost nobody in the United States can reasonably favor. Having gone through the enormous cost of arresting inflation by the 1982 recession, it seems absurd to risk bringing it back by unwise fiscal policies. For the long run, as the evidence on deficient capital formation in the previous chapter showed, the United States is in no position to make such a dramatic and drastic reduction in its capital investment. Chapter 1 showed the deficits do not consist of higher levels of public capital formation. Private saving rates have been remarkably stable as government deficits have increased, so there seems to be little Barro-like offset. Should these patterns persist, the country will either end up with a lower capital stock, or with a large share of its capital owned by foreigners. Future living standards will be reduced, here and perhaps also abroad.

WINNERS AND LOSERS

One of the interesting features of economic policy making is that economies are so large and diverse that no matter how unwise a particular policy seems to be from the standpoint of the nation as a whole, it will almost certainly benefit certain groups and hurt others. It may then be instructive to inspect the likely pattern of gains and losses from the deficits. Who wins and who loses?

Starting with the short run, the deficits will drive up interest rates and raise the value of the dollar. Both shifts divert productive resources from capital formation to present-day consumption, and on the production side, both will help industries producing consumer goods and hurt industries that produce investment goods, exports, or compete with imports. The main industries that suffer from such a shift are housing, the most volatile component of investment; agriculture, potentially one of the United States' strong export industries; old-line manufacturing industries such as steel, which compete with imports and produce capital equipment; and autos and textiles, which compete with imports. The troubles of each industry are well known, and are often reported in the newspapers and on television. Although management problems, high wages, and natural obsolescence may be present in each industry, the fact that the dollar has risen sharply, almost 50 percent against a trade-weighted average of foreign currencies between 1981 and 1983, has greatly aggravated the basic problems. To a very large degree, America's industrialization problems may really be dollar-overvaluation problems, directly attributable to budget deficits.[5]

There is a regional dimension to the problem, too. Again, to a large degree the industries suffering most during the recession and subsequent recovery are concentrated in a band starting at the north in the Great Lakes region and proceeding down the east bank of the Mississippi River. States benefitting from the shift are located on the west bank of the Mississippi, in the southwest, and in New England. States such as Michigan, Illinois, Ohio, Pennsylvania, West Virginia, Kentucky, Tennessee, and Mississippi all had unemployment rates in excess of 11 percent in 1983 (when the national rate was 9.5 percent); states such as Texas, Arizona, New York, Massachusetts, and Connecticut had unemployment rates below 8 percent.[6] This diversity in economic conditions had not been experienced earlier in the postwar period, and though the causes are not well understood, it is certainly possible that the highly expansionary fiscal policy and its concomitant imbalances was an important contributing factor. Whether or not Horace Greeley's advice for young men to go west was appropriate when it was originally uttered in the 1880s, it certainly seems appropriate for young workers one hundred years later.

There are also noteworthy gains and losses pertaining to our long-run analysis. Here the big gainers are those in the present generation who experience a rise in the share of output devoted to consumption; the losers are those in the future who suffer from the fact that the nation is bequeathing less capital. To illustrate these shifts, Fig. 2.2 shows the historical time series of real consumption per capita from 1950 to 1983, with the main fluctuations in the series illustrated. It then shows a standard future forecast up to the year 2010, with per capita real consumption growing at its average rate for the past decade, adjusted downward slightly to account for the declining growth in the labor force expected for the next two decades. This base case is labeled the "No Deficits" scenario. The dotted line then gives the path of consumption if the large deficits come to pass. Referring to Appendix B, in the 1970s the share of output devoted to capital formation averaged 11 percent, the economy's overall growth rate 2.5 percent, and the capital-labor ratio was 4.4 times output per worker. As a result of the higher structural deficits, in the 1980s the saving share should be reduced to about 8.5 percent, output per worker will drop about 9 percent, and the capital-labor ratio will ultimately drop almost 30 percent.[7] Consumption will first rise above the No Deficits path as

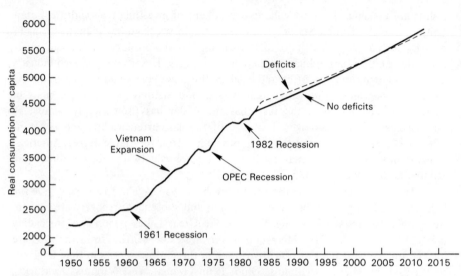

FIGURE 2.2   U.S. Consumption Per Capita (1972 $), 1950–2015.

Source: *The Economic Report of the President, February, 1984,* Table B.24; Edward M. Gramlich, "How Bad Are the Large Deficits?" in Greg B. Mills and John L. Palmer (eds.), *Federal Budget Policy in the 1980s,* The Urban Institute, Washington, D.C., 1984.

resources are used to produce consumption goods, and then drop back down as the gradual erosion in the amount of capital per worker leads to lower production and output than would otherwise be the case. Figure 2.2 shows the pattern of this drop.

Figure 2.2 also shows the remarkable fact, well known to those who work with growth models, that the size of the existing capital stock is so large relative to new capital formation that it takes a very long time for the deficits to do their damage. In the simulation it is nearly twenty years before aggregate consumption declines, and because they benefit from earlier rises in consumption, households in every age class over thirty will benefit from the deficits. Although these particular dates vary according to a series of technical assumptions that must be made in running the simulations, all of these assumptions are realistic; even attempts to vary the assumptions to make earlier the day of reckoning imply that consumption will remain high for many years and that most living American adults will benefit from these deficits. In other words, it is possible for the present generation of American adults to create for itself a consumption "high" that lasts for an extremely long time by the simple expedient of running large deficits. The costs will be left for our children and their children. If the anticipated deficits actually do occur and the standard growth of consumption per capita slackens just a bit, our generation could even have the dubious distinction of being the first in United States history that will actually have higher living standards than its children.[8]

Therefore, even though the continued structural deficits, in provoking such a sharp drop in capital formation, seem harmful to most observers, a careful analysis of them demonstrates even more disturbing shifts than might be imagined. Within the present generation, the deficits appear to be largely responsible for a shift in spending propensities that may be wiping out whole industries and harming broad groups of states on one side of the Mississippi, to the gain of those on the other. Across generations, the present generation of adults is in effect stealing capital from its children in an unprecedented manner, through policies that the children cannot vote on. One shift causes major dislocations; the other is clearly undemocratic and seems unethical.

NOTES

[1] These matters are nicely described in Arthur M. Okun, *Prices and Quantities: A Macroeconomic Analysis*, The Brookings Institution, Washington, D.C., 1981.

[2] These broad statements have been confirmed in any number of more careful econometric analyses. One recent example is Robert J. Gordon, "Price Inertia and Policy Ineffectiveness in the United States, 1890–1980," *The Journal of Political Economy*, vol. 90, December, 1982, pp. 1087–1117.

[3] The analysis here is trickier than it might seem. When all prices and wages change together, there is no necessary stimulus to demand because all economic actors have constant real incomes and face constant relative prices. What eventually stimulates demand (when prices fall) is that the stock of money-fixed assets now stretches farther and makes people spend more through a wealth effect. Also, if prices in other countries are fixed, our goods are less expensive, and net exports will rise.

[4] The first economists to explain this important point in depth were Robert A. Mundell, in "Capital Mobility and Stabilization Policy under Fixed and Flexible Exchange Rates," *Canadian Journal of Economics and Political Science*, vol. 29, November, 1963, pp. 475–485; and Marcus Fleming, *Domestic Financial Plans Under Fixed and Flexible Exchange Rates*, International Monetary Fund Staff Papers, Washington, D.C., 1962.

[5] These matters are thoroughly discussed in *The Economic Report of the President, February 1984*, Chapter 3; and Alice M. Rivlin (ed.), *Economic Choices*, The Brookings Institution, Washington, D.C., 1984, Chapter 6.

[6] A more complete analysis of these movements is given by James Medoff, "U.S. Labor Markets: Imbalance, Wage Growth, and Productivity in the 1970s," in *Brookings Papers on Economic Activity*, 1: 1983, pp. 87–128.

[7] The simulations on which these and other numbers are based are described in Edward M. Gramlich, "How Bad are the Large Deficits?" in Greg B. Mills and John L. Palmer (eds.), *Federal Budget Policy in the 1980s*, The Urban Institute, Washington, D.C., 1984. There are a number of behavioral assumptions one must make in running such simulations; for plotting Fig. 2.2, we used only the basic case.

[8] Because this distinction would be a dubious one indeed, it may be well to spell out the conditions necessary for its occurrence. Figure 2.2 establishes the nor-

mal case by assuming that consumption per capita grows at 1 percent per year for the next decade and a half. This rate is slightly *below* the rate of growth of real per capita consumption for the past decade and much *above* the rate of growth of real GNP per worker over the same period. There are three reasons for the difference, all of which may be temporary:

1. Consumption has grown more than GNP because the deficits occurring have already crowded out domestic investment. In Fig. 2.2, we project these deficits to get no larger.
2. Consumption has grown more than GNP because the deficits have raised the value of the dollar and caused a rising trade deficit. This phenomenon cannot go on forever.
3. The number of workers has grown more than the number of people, because of the well-known extraordinary increases in numbers of teenage and female workers. These extraordinary increases may not continue either.

If all of these trends stop, and the productivity slowdown in GNP growth does not stop, we should be extrapolating much lower future increases for real consumption per capita, even in the no deficits case. In this case, the assumed normal rate of increase of consumption per capita could approach the low rate of increase of GNP per worker and the speculation in the text could prove to be correct. Whether it actually turns out to be correct or not (we will be dead by then and so may you), the fact that it is a live possibility is disturbing enough.

CHAPTER THREE
INTEREST PAYMENTS:
THE TICKING TIME BOMB

The existence of deficits means, by definition, that the government is not paying for some of its expenditures. In the previous two chapters we saw how these deficits are reflected in negative values for Sg, the public saving component of the overall saving-investment identity. If not offset by private saving increases, these deficits ultimately lead to a reduction in the capital-labor ratio of the economy and in the economy's total consumption possibilities, through the growth model process described.

But that is not the end of it. An analysis that focuses only on Sg does not bring in the financial side of government deficits. In order to pay for the goods and services not covered by available tax revenues, the government must get the cash somewhere. If it already had the funds in its own checking account, it would just run down this balance and that would be that. But like most private households, the government keeps a relatively small amount in its own checking account, not nearly enough to cover $200 billion worth of deficits. To come up with this kind of money, more fundamental actions are necessary.

One such action is for the government to print the money. The Treasury is not actually empowered to print money, but it is possible to achieve the same effect through the existence of the Federal Reserve, the nation's central bank. The government can borrow from the private sector by floating interest-bearing bonds. The "Fed" can then buy up these bonds (offering private investors a higher price) by creating reserve accounts for the credit of the appropriate banks and wealth holders. These reserve accounts form the base of the nation's money supply and are used by banks to expand the money supply through what is known as the *deposit-creation multiplier*. The entire transaction results in the deficits being financed by an expansion of the money supply, or "monetized" in the jargon of central bankers.

This method of financing deficits seems beguilingly simple, almost magical. In many less-developed countries where private capital markets are undeveloped and government bonds have a poor default risk history, this is the way government deficits are financed. But in the United States only a very small share of the government deficit is typically monetized, a practice that can be expected to continue. The reason is inflation. Monetization of the entire $200 billion deficit, with multiple expansion of the money supply on top of that, would result in an enormous increase in the supply of money. It would certainly lead to rapid expansion of spending and to rapid inflation. The main present-day responsibility of the "Fed" is to limit inflation by controlling the growth of the money supply, and it has always taken this responsibility very seriously. Legally it cannot buy the newly floated interest-bearing obligations of the federal government (beyond a very trivial amount), and for the most part it simply will not. The result is that the growth of the money supply has generally been kept to the low level dictated by the need to control inflation, and the vast majority of the government's interest-bearing obligations have stayed with the private sector.

The implications of accumulations of private holdings of interest-bearing government securities are fairly obvious. Interest payments, already an important component of government spending, will rise. Not only do they rise because the stock of bonds grows with the cumulated flow of deficits, but if, as we have seen, the governmental dissaving drives up interest rates, interest payments rise again. The higher level of interest payments leads to a vicious circle of budget deficits—deficits raise debt, which raises interest payments, which raises government spending, which raises deficits. Given this vicious circle, once a certain level of deficits has been attained, it becomes much harder for the government to hold the deficits even to that level. This vicious circle represents the ticking time bomb of the deficit problem; even as we read about present deficits, forces are at work to make future deficits larger.

In this chapter we focus on these issues. We first review the accounting conventions, examining both the effect of interest payments on the expenditure side of the government budget and the ways of financing deficits. We then fill out this discussion with some numbers that show how large interest payments are now and how they, and the deficits, are growing under present policies. We conclude by discussing two old-time conceptual issues pertaining to debts and deficits—whether a government debt should be thought of as internal or external to a country, and whether there is a burden to this debt.

FINANCING THE DEFICITS

As was done in Chapter 1, we can illustrate the facts of debts and deficits by examining present-day numbers. The relevant ones are shown in Table 3.1. The top panel of the table shows the official budget deficit to be $195 billion in fiscal

TABLE 3.1 Financing the U.S. Budget Deficit in Fiscal Year 1983

	BILLIONS CURRENT $
INCOME-FLOW SIDE	
Official budget deficit	195
Noninterest component	(104)
Interest payments	(91)
FINANCIAL SIDE	
Official budget deficit	195
Off-budget outlays	(12)
Increase in cash balances	(5)
Gross borrowing	212
Borrowing from the "Fed"	(−21)
Borrowing from the private sector	191

Source: *Budget of the U.S. Government, Fiscal Year, 1985,* Special Analysis E, Tables E-1 and E-2; *The Economic Report of the President, February, 1984,* Table B.76.

1983, exactly the same as in Table 1.2 on page 8. Of this $195 billion, slightly less than half, $91 billion, represents interest payments. The rest represents the difference between normal expenditures and taxes. If it were possible to eliminate the outstanding government debt by a stroke of the pen—something occasionally tried in countries after a political revolution—the present government deficit could be cut almost in half.[1]

On the financial side, gross government borrowing was $17 billion more than the official budget deficit in 1983. Of this total, $12 billion consists of loans the federal government made to "off-budget" agencies for farm credit, mortgage insurance, and higher education. These loans are off-budget because, as stated above, they represent only asset transactions with the private sector, not income flows. But they do have to be added in here because they raise the amount of total borrowing done by the Treasury Department. By the same token, when the government builds up its checking account balance, as it did to the tune of $5 billion in 1983, gross borrowing needs also rise.

Of the gross borrowing total of $212 billion, $21 billion (10 percent) was repurchased by the "Fed" to generate normal expansion in the money supply. We said earlier that the "Fed" will not expand its open market purchases of government bonds simply to finance the deficit, but it *will* normally take up some of these securities to permit the money supply to expand somewhat, as it must in a growing economy. In 1983 the "Fed" purchases for money supply creation approximately balanced the difference between the official deficit and gross borrowing—hence gross borrowing from the private sector (excluding the "Fed") was only $4 billion different from the official deficit.

The dynamics of the relationship among debt, deficits, and interest can now be summarized with a simple equation. To keep things simple, we assume that normal "Fed" open market purchases of securities for money growth exactly equal the normal accretion in the government's cash balance and the normal growth of its net loans to farmers, homeowners, and college students. Then the identities shown in Table 3.1 can be expressed in nominal terms as

$$dD = G - T + iD \qquad (1)$$

where D refers to the stock of government interest-bearing debt; dD refers to the change in this stock, or just the government deficit under our simplifying assumption; G refers to government purchases of goods and services, just as in Chapter 1; T refers to taxes less transfer payments, just as in Chapter 1; and i is the economy-wide nominal interest rate. Nominal interest payments are then equal to iD.[2]

In a strict sense, the vicious circle described above comes about whenever dD is positive—in this case, D will grow, interest payments will grow, too, and the deficit, dD, will grow, also. But surely simply pointing to growth in interest payments is being alarmist—in the growth models we looked at in Appendix B in our discussion in the previous chapter, everything is growing in a growing economy. Hence the true vicious-circle test should be to determine whether the dynamics of this financial link imply that debt and deficits are growing *relative* to GNP.

The growth rate of the government's interest-bearing debt can be determined by dividing through (1) by the stock of debt D, giving

$$dD/D = (G - T)/D + i \qquad (2)$$

where the left-hand side of (2) now is exactly the rate of change of government debt. If G = T, it can be seen that the first term on the right-hand side drops out, and the rate of growth of government debt is just the nominal interest rate i. In this case, the question of whether the debt growing at rate i is outpacing the economy is simply whether the interest rate exceeds the economy's growth rate, also in nominal terms. Recalling the growth analysis in Chapter 2, and particularly referring to Appendix B, the answer is "yes" for all economies that are saving less than the long-run consumption-maximizing amount, as the U.S. economy clearly is. Even in this case, U.S. deficits are large enough to inspire concern about the vicious circle— deficits and debt will grow relative to GNP unless something is done about either G or T.[3]

But in the United States at present the situation is even worse, because as Table 3.1 shows, G also exceeds T. More than half of present-day U.S. deficits have nothing to do with interest payments, implying that the rate of change of government debt is more than twice as high as the growth rate of the economy. Under these circumstances, our vicious circle will become even more vicious very quickly.

To see just how quickly, we give a simple calculation based on present-day data. We set the nominal interest rate and (G − T)/D at their fiscal 1984 values (9 percent and 4.6 percent, respectively). We then use the inflation, real interest rate, and GNP growth forecast of the Congressional Budget Office to compute values for equation (2) on to the year 2000. We measure the deficit for one year, add this deficit to the previous stock of debt to get the new stock, measure interest payments and deficits next year, and so forth. The resulting deficit and debt numbers are divided by nominal GNP (from the CBO) and are shown in Fig. 3.1.

The results are anything but reassuring. As Fig. 3.1 shows, in fiscal 1984, the start of the simulation, the deficit to GNP ratio was already 4.6 percent, much larger than its historical average (see Fig. 1.1 on page 14). Most of this change was brought about mainly by the non-interest part of the deficit, which rose by 2.5 percentage points between fiscal 1981 and fiscal 1984. But even assuming this growth to be arrested and interest rates to climb no further, as we do, the vicious circle has now started. The deficit–GNP ratio rises inexorably to 5.7 percent by 1990, to 6.6 percent by 1995, and so forth. The debt-GNP ratio was only 27 percent in fiscal 1981, but it rises to 40 percent by fiscal 1984, to 52 percent by 1990, and to 63 percent by 1995. The ratio has taken off.

These projections are not meant as predictions, for Congress may actually change G or T. But they do show that unless some changes are made—the most obvious being that the non-interest component of the deficit must be cut radically, and quickly—it will be impossible to avoid a progressive increase in the deficit and a progressive reduction in the share of output devoted to capital formation. It was not interest payments that got the deficits started, but now that the deficits exist, interest payments provide the momentum to keep them high and rising. That is the essence of a vicious circle.

FIGURE 3.1 Federal Debt and Deficits Relative to GNP. Projected, 1985 –2000 (No Policy Changes).

Source: 1984 values and projections of GNP, prices, and interest rates are from Congressional Budget Office, *The Economic and Budget Outlook: An Update,* August, 1984, Tables I-2 and III-8.

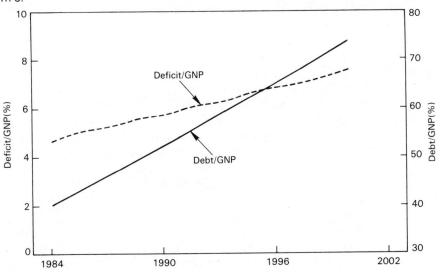

IS THERE A BURDEN TO THE DEBT?

We conclude this discussion of interest, deficits, and debt by returning to two conceptual issues that have long bothered economists. The first involves the question of whether government debt should be treated as internal or external; the second is the question of whether there is a burden to the debt.

The internal–external argument has arisen in connection with federal versus state fiscal issues and now national versus international debt. An often-heard argument is that it is all right for the federal government to run deficits because the interest payments are not true payments but simply transfer payments from taxpayers to bondholders, with all of the income staying in the country. For state governments, on the other hand, the argument is just the reverse: Because the taxpayers pay interest to bondholders who generally live outside the state in question, most of this debt is external and its costs are real. Exactly the same argument would be applied to national debt, if the bondholders lived outside the country.

We find no flaws with the second half of the argument, but we do with the first. On the second half, external holding of debt clearly does mean that interest payments impose a real cost on taxpayers, effectively assessing a service charge for capital used by whatever government is making the interest payment. Whatever the stabilization value of budget deficits at the state level, one's overall evaluation of these deficits must include the real costs represented by interest payments.

Where the common argument runs into trouble involves government debt that is nominally internal—in the case at hand, U.S. government debt held by, and paying interest to, U.S. citizens. Should this debt be viewed differently from external debt?

The answer to the question brings up a matter that often distinguishes economists from others. It might seem logical to trace the flow of interest payments, find them to travel from some citizens to other citizens, and argue that there is no real cost to these interest payments. Economists would ask one more question: How much better off are the recipients of the interest? If they are not much better off, the payments cost some citizens but do not benefit others, and should be viewed as costly.

In the case of debt and borrowing, almost all observers claim that financial assets are traded on a national or world capital market with high elasticities of supply. If the interest rate on a particular asset were lowered slightly, there are so many close substitutes that nobody would hold the asset. What this means is that all bondholders, whether they live in the United States or Saudi Arabia, receive the same real interest rate on their assets, and they will receive approximately this rate whether they hold the debt of the U.S. government or the debt of any number of other institutions with similar maturity and risk characteristics. This in turn means that although U.S. taxpayers do indeed suffer when they make interest payments, U.S. bondholders are not much better off—they would have earned approximately the real interest rate whether they held the U.S. bond and got its interest, or some other bond and got its interest. In this sense, even U.S. debt that is held internally has economic costs that are just like that of external debt, and it should really be viewed very much like external debt.[4]

The answer to the internal–external question more or less provides the answer to the related question of the burden of the government's debt. If it were to be internal, with the interest being simply a transfer between two groups of citizens, there would be no obvious burden from the debt. But with an effectively external debt, the burden is clear. Interest payments represent payments by present taxpayers for debt accumulated some time in the past. If this debt is expanded through new deficits, future interest payments will rise and impose costs on future generations. Looking at this another way in keeping with the growth analysis of the previous chapter, there is a burden of the government debt if the process of accumulating this debt through deficits lowers aggregate capital formation. In this sense, the governmental dissaving of present taxpayers (unless offset by higher private saving) lowers either the capital stock bequeathed to the future or owned by Americans, lowers future living standards, and clearly does entail a burden.[5]

NOTES

[1] This is, of course, not a serious suggestion. And even if it were possible, it would not be as beneficial as might be thought. Many of the pension funds holding the retirement assets of our parents or ourselves have government bonds as their main assets. Many of the banks and savings-and-loan associations holding our deposits also hold large quantities of government bonds.

[2] We write (1) in nominal terms because that is what corresponds to Table 3.1. In using (1) to see how real debt levels change over time, or debt relative to GNP changes over time, we would get the same answer if we had written the expression in real terms using the real interest rate to measure interest payments, as is required in the Eisner–Pieper measure of the deficit given in Chapter 1.

[3] To see this, in nominal terms the debt is growing at the rate of $(G-T)/D + r + p$, where r is the real interest rate and p the rate of inflation. GNP is growing at the rate of $n + p$, where n is the normal real growth rate of the economy. Even if $G = T$, debt is growing at a rate greater than GNP if $r > n$.

[4] For those who have some background in microeconomics, the argument we make here says that when the supply of funds to the government is highly elastic, there will be no, or very little, producer surplus generated by the outward shift in the government's demand for funds. There is also a real-world phenomenon that is beginning to make the case even clearer. Increasingly, the open worldwide capital market spoken of above means that, in fact, foreigners are beginning to hold large quantities of U.S. debt. By fiscal 1983, *Budget of the U.S. Government, Fiscal Year, 1985,* Special Analysis E, reports that foreigners held about 15 percent of the outstanding federal debt, and the press reports that the U.S. Treasury is now trying to sell even more of the new debt abroad.

[5] This argument was first stated formally by Franco Modigliani, "Long Run Implications of Alternative Fiscal Policies and the Burden of the National Debt," *The Economic Journal,* vol. 71, December, 1961, pp. 730–755.

CHAPTER FOUR
REDUCING THE DEFICIT: EXPENDITURES

Up to this point, we have analyzed the deficit as a summary measure of the macro-economic impact of the federal budget. Both its present and future level seem clearly too large from this standpoint. Now we get to the hard question: How can the government cut the deficit? We deal with the expenditure side of the budget here and the tax side in the next chapter.

To avoid unnecessary tedium, we do not give a line-by-line analysis of all the many types of federal spending. We stick to fairly broad categories and use the projections of the impartial Congressional Budget Office (CBO) to get a feel for the expenditure-reducing possibilities. Throughout the analysis we implicitly assume that the broad outlines of what the government does are not likely to change—one could always make very drastic reductions in government spending by proposing drastic restrictions in underlying governmental responsibilities. Instead, we are looking for cases where programs no longer serve their original purpose, or where there are management efficiencies that might reduce outlays without interfering with the basic goals of government spending. As is natural, we will also focus more intensively on types of spending that can make a difference—ones "where the money is," in Willie Sutton's famous phrase.

For the reader who wants to skip the details and take our word for it, the news is not good. Following the substantial cuts in domestic spending made during the last few years, about exactly matched by rises in defense spending, there seems to be no way that the deficit can be eliminated by spending changes in the foreseeable future without radical changes in a conception of what the federal government should do. And by radical changes, we mean exactly that. One such radical change—

to eliminate all domestic spending aimed at helping the poor—would not be nearly enough. Even eliminating all such spending plus all education and training programs would not be nearly enough. And cutting the defense budget in half would not be enough. We are talking about big changes indeed.

Throughout the analysis, we focus on the CBO's baseline budget forecasts for fiscal year 1990. These estimates are not forecasts as such. Over such a long period it is impossible to make realistic forecasts. But it is not impossible to determine the implications of present policies, if they stay in place. Hence the estimates, for what is known as the *current services (policy) budget,* show what would happen if currently legislated tax and expenditure programs were to stay in place. The dollar numbers then change only because of price changes, demographic changes, and other changes that are assumed to be independent of the budget forecasts. In these forecasts, defense spending is assumed to grow at the annual rate of about 5 percent in real terms (the inflation rate plus 5 percent in money terms), and most other types of discretionary domestic spending are assumed to remain the same in real terms.

CBO's economic projections show GNP being very close to its high employment level by 1990. Thus the 1990 figures used here are measured at close to high employment levels, and allow us to look at something like the "structural" budget deficit defined in Chapter 1, abstracting from any cyclical phenomena that might occur between now and then. Moreover, as we write in the spring of 1985, 1990 is far enough away so that measures designed to reduce the deficit will have time to take effect. One does not expect the deficit to vanish overnight, but given the analysis of the preceding chapters, five years would seem to be a reasonable amount of time to straighten out the deficit problem.

The problem is, as we have said, large. According to the CBO, the unified budget deficit in fiscal 1990 will be $290 billion, 5.2 percent of GNP. Revenues are projected at $1088 billion (19.4 percent of GNP) and outlays are projected at $1378 billion (24.6 percent of GNP). Our discussion in earlier chapters indicated that if society were to try to save at the rate that maximized per capita standards of living over time, the 1990 deficit should be zero or negative (that is, there should be a surplus). The question for this chapter is how to achieve that.

There are many ways to divide up the federal budget. For our purposes, it makes the most sense to use the CBO categories, shown in Table 4.1 for 1970, 1980, 1985, along with projections for 1988 and 1990. (See also Fig. 4.1.) A striking feature of Table 4.1 is that the first four major categories, social insurance, defense, interest, and federal employees' retirement and disability programs, nearly exhausted revenues in 1985 (had the government done nothing else, there would have been a surplus of $38 billion) and more than exhaust revenues in 1990 (if the government did nothing else, the deficit would be $18 billion). Also striking is the fact that interest on the federal debt accounts for about 80 percent of the deficit by 1990, illustrating the vicious circle we talked about in Chapter 3. The only known way to reduce interest payments is to reduce deficits themselves.

TABLE 4.1 Composition of Actual and Projected Federal Outlays, Selected Fiscal Years 1970–1990 (in billions of current dollars and as a percent of GNP in parentheses)

	1970	1980	1985	1988	1990
Social Insurance Programs	41	174	276	342	397
	(4.2)	(6.7)	(7.2)	(7.1)	(7.1)
Social Security and Railroad Retirement	31	122	190	230	260
	(3.2)	(4.7)	(4.9)	(4.8)	(4.6)
Medicare	7	34	69	95	119
	(0.7)	(1.3)	(1.8)	(2.0)	(2.1)
Unemployment Compensation	3	18	17	17	18
	(0.3)	(0.7)	(0.4)	(0.4)	(0.3)
Defense	82	134	252	347	424
	(8.4)	(5.2)	(6.5)	(7.2)	(7.6)
Net Interest	14	53	130	186	230
	(1.5)	(2.0)	(3.4)	(3.9)	(4.1)
Federal Employees' Retirement and Disability	6	26	39	48	55
	(0.6)	(1.0)	(1.0)	(1.0)	(1.0)
Civilian	3	15	23	28	32
	(0.3)	(0.6)	(0.6)	(0.6)	(0.6)
Military	3	11	16	20	23
	(0.3)	(0.4)	(0.4)	(0.4)	(0.4)
Means-Tested Programs	10	47	66	77	84
	(1.1)	(1.8)	(1.7)	(1.6)	(1.5)
Food Stamps	1	9	12	13	14
	(0.1)	(0.3)	(0.3)	(0.3)	(0.2)
Medicaid	3	14	22	28	33
	(0.3)	(0.5)	(0.6)	(0.6)	(0.6)
Other	6	24	32	36	37
	(0.6)	(0.9)	(0.8)	(0.7)	(0.7)
Other Federal Programs	43	144	174	174	184
	(4.4)	(5.5)	(4.5)	(3.6)	(3.3)
"Mandatory" Programs	11	33	54	42	41
	(1.1)	(1.3)	(1.4)	(0.9)	(0.7)
"Discretionary" Programs	44	141	168	191	211
	(4.5)	(5.5)	(4.4)	(4.0)	(3.8)
Offsetting Budget Receipts	−12	−30	−48	−59	−65
	(−1.2)	(−1.2)	(−1.2)	(−1.2)	(−1.2)
Total Unified Budget Outlays	196	577	938	1174	1378
	(20.2)	(22.4)	(24.3)	(24.3)	(24.6)

Note: Details may not add to totals because of rounding.

Source: Expenditure and GNP projections for 1985, 1988, and 1990 are from Congressional Budget Office, *The Economic and Budget Outlook: Fiscal Years 1986–1990*, February, 1985, Tables I-11, II-1, II-2, II-5, and II-6; 1970 and 1980 data are from Tables E-5, E-6, and E-8, with detail for some 1970 and 1980 means-tested and retirement programs taken from *Budget of the U.S. Government, Fiscal Year, 1972, and Fiscal Year, 1982.*

SOCIAL INSURANCE PROGRAMS

Social insurance programs, of which social security is by far the largest, account for 7.1 percent of GNP in 1990, down from 7.2 percent in 1985. The slowing in the growth of these programs can be largely attributed to the 1983 social security amendments, which reduced outlays somewhat, and to the improved economy in

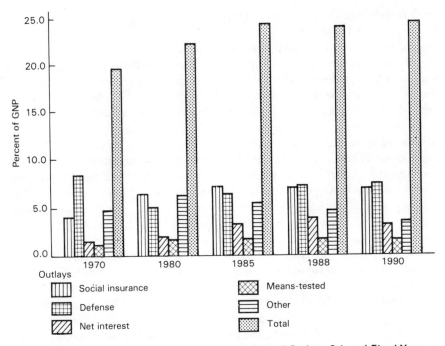

FIGURE 4.1 Composition of Actual and Projected Federal Outlays, Selected Fiscal Years, as a Percent of GNP.

1990, which will lead to lower unemployment compensation and somewhat lower social security payments. Even so, social insurance programs are currently the largest single category of outlays, and even after the rapid defense buildup expected for the remainder this decade, will run a close second to defense in 1990. In spite of these numbers, social insurance programs are not a key element of the deficit problem. The reason is that they carry their own earmarked taxes with them, and with the exception of medicare, the taxes, at least over the long run, roughly cover expenditures.

Social Security

As mentioned above, social security differs from most programs in that it has its own earmarked payroll tax. The revenues from this tax go into a special trust fund that finances benefit payments. Over the long run, the program is designed to be self-financing in the sense that anticipated trust fund revenues should cover expected outlays. In the late 1970s and early 1980s, the system was plainly out of balance—expenditures exceeded revenues for a number of years. Had nothing been done, the trust fund would have been exhausted, and revenues would have been insufficient to cover benefits sometime in 1984. Following legislative changes made in 1983, the system is once again in balance. It is projected to run surpluses for the remainder of this century, and slowly shift toward deficits as the baby-boom generation retires. Although a period of adverse economic performance, such as that which precipitated the recent crisis, might again put the system in some jeopardy, the currently legislated tax rates (and future increases) should cover benefits for a long period to come. Thus, as of now, the program does reduce the deficit.

This should not be taken to mean that changes in the social security system should not be considered in the context of a concern with economic growth, which is what leads us to worry about the deficit in the first place. In fact, we argued earlier that our major reason for being troubled by the current and prospective deficits is that they represent a consumption binge for those currently living, to be paid for by their children and grandchildren. Social security is a program under which those currently working directly support those now retired (or disabled). Moreover, the level of benefits received by current recipients of social security far exceeds the amount that their taxes could have accumulated had they been invested in private pension plans. There may well be an argument, then, for reducing social security benefits below what is currently scheduled, leaving payroll tax rates unchanged and increasing the contribution of social security to aggregate saving and capital formation. Alternatively, both legislated benefits and taxes could be reduced somewhat, and another tax raised, with the same consequences for the deficit. Perhaps $20 billion of budget savings could be realized under such a scheme.

Unlike essentially all private pension programs, social security benefits are fully indexed for inflation—their purchasing power stays constant throughout the life of the beneficiary. Under the 1983 amendments, if wages rise slower than prices (as they did during the late 1970s and early 1980s, but as they have never before done in U.S. history), benefits are indexed by wages, so that social security recipients would share with the working population the costs of declining real incomes. Indexing could be limited further, but such a change would put those who depend on social security for the bulk of their retirement incomes in the position of having their real incomes erode over the entire period of their retirement. Given the purposes of the social security program, this does not seem to be good public policy if maintained over very long periods of time. The program is designed to replace income lost due to retirement or disability, and once the initial size of the replacement is determined, it seems reasonable that its purchasing power remain at least roughly constant, subject to the caveat that everyone shares in hard times, as will be the case under current law.

Medicare

Medicare is like social security in that it carries its own tax with it, but is unlike social security in that currently legislated tax levels will not cover future expected payouts. This is because part of the program (Medicare Part B) is paid for out of general revenues, and also because program outlays are increasing as a share of GNP and are projected to continue doing so. Indeed, by the 1990s medicare is projected to run a deficit that is larger than social security's surplus. Moreover, it is generally conceded that currently legislated tax rates fall far short of what is necessary to make medicare solvent over the long run, even with some recent changes that have tightened up on the procedures for reimbursing hospitals.

The CBO's baseline projections assume that real costs per hospital admission will increase at only 0.25 percent per year more than the cost of goods and services bought by hospitals. Thus there will be no improvement in 1990 baseline deficit, even if this ambitious target is achieved. Thus, both in the short and longer terms, medicare does make a significant positive contribution to the deficit. Indeed, although little has been said publicly on the matter, the rate at which medicare expenditures have been growing, coupled with the aging of the population that will continue to occur over the coming decades, leads us to question whether publicly provided private-style medical insurance for the elderly is something that the society can afford over the long run. To the extent that the new reimbursement mechanism is successful, it may be possible to continue medicare without major program revisions, but even under this rather optimistic assumption, the medicare trust fund will be in deficit by about $100 billion in the late 1990s. There is nothing in current law or projections to alleviate the problem in the foreseeable future.

Over the long run, it is essential that medicare outlays be further curbed (perhaps by making the program cover catastrophic illness only, reducing coverage for relatively minor ailments and requiring larger co-payments on the part of beneficiaries), or that the legislated tax rates increase, or both. Society's concern about providing medical care to the elderly is certainly appropriate, but given that medicare has its own earmarked tax, it is not clear why we have built into the forseeable future a program whose outlays will not be covered by the tax. If the principle that taxes roughly cover outlays is adopted for medicare (as it has been for social security), the effect of medicare on the deficit would be important. As things stand now, even with the optimistic CBO assumptions, the deficit in medicare will be about 0.9 percent of GNP, or about one-sixth of the total deficit, in 1990. With more pessimistic assumptions, the impact could be much larger. Although the social issues raised by changing medicare are difficult ones, merely getting society to take the long-term deficit in medicare seriously would be considerable progress.

DEFENSE

According to the CBO baseline projections, defense will be the largest single category of federal expenditures by 1990. Currently, it runs a close second to social insurance programs. We claim no special expertise in analysis of defense programs, and much of our discussion of defense spending is taken from the work of others, especially William W. Kaufmann.[2] Before going into a discussion of possibilities for reducing the defense budget, however, it will be valuable to view defense spending in light of our discussion on budget concepts in Chapter 1. In particular, we are interested in the extent to which defense spending is best viewed as consumption or investment, and thus the extent to which it is appropriate to have it paid for by current taxpayers or future taxpayers.

Is Defense Spending Current Consumption?

Special Analysis D of the *Budget of the United States Government for Fiscal Year, 1985* shows that 43 percent of defense outlays can be thought of as capital acquisitions—that is, as purchases of goods and services that yield benefits over a long period of time. The bulk of these goods and services are physical equipment (such as weapons systems and construction) and research and development. Going further, if one views the purpose of defense spending as the securing of a future for the society, it can be argued that to the extent that defense spending contributes positively to the probability that the United States will be an independent nation able to enjoy the fruits of her heritage, *all* of defense spending might appropriately be viewed as investment rather than consumption.

In order to permit us to focus on the issue of whether defense spending is best thought of as consumption or investment, it is necessary to construct a rather simplified and stylized example, one that permits abstraction from many of the real-world issues raised by the defense budget. Once we have the simplified framework in hand, we can go back to the more complicated case.

Consider a country that has a certain stock of wealth and that produces income in a given year. The country faces a threat to its wealth and its future income—there are outside invaders that might try to steal the wealth and appropriate some share of the income. The country must allocate its current resources among three activities—consumption, productive investment, and defense spending. This last category is designed to make it costly for the invaders to engage in theft, and thus to protect both current and future consumption for the citizens of the country. To keep things simple, suppose that the only type of defense spending that is used is current expenditure—the employment of soldiers who guard the country's borders. And to make things even simpler, let us assume that there is no uncertainty in the situation. The amount that will be stolen from the country in any given year decreases as defense expenditures rise. Following the law of decreasing returns, the reduction in theft per dollar of defense spending might also be assumed to decrease as defense spending rises.

Under these idealized circumstances, the optimal level of defense spending is determined by an economist's marginal condition: Such spending should be undertaken until the last dollar of spending reduces theft by exactly one dollar. Note that at this point the level of theft is not zero (a complete defense is not optimal). Rather, the cost of reducing further theft is greater than the gain. In addition, under these simplified assumptions, defense spending will be investment in proportion to the amount that society engages in investment. At the margin, one dollar's worth of defense will save society one dollar's worth of wealth, and that dollar of wealth will be allocated to consumption and investment like any other dollar would be. Thus, if the country devotes about 12 percent of net output to capital accumulation, about 12 percent of defense spending can be seen as investment.

Unfortunately, the actual situation with defense spending is substantially more complicated. One key characteristic of defense spending, especially in the modern world, is that it is designed to reduce the probability of fundamental long-term changes in the nature of the world. In the extreme, the world as we know it could cease to exist. Less extreme, but still very much of concern to the Defense Department, is the possibility that a lack of military power will cause reductions in the ability of the United States to make use of its own resources. Moreover, there is no fixed relationship between defense spending and the degree to which U.S. wealth might be made unavailable to the population by invaders. It is the purpose of defense spending to make such events less likely. Additionally, much defense spending is for hardware that lasts a long time, rather than for personnel or equipment that is used up in the year that it is purchased. Finally, there is the possibility, raised by many commentators, that some defense spending *increases* the probability of that nuclear war, leading to the loss of essentially all wealth (not to mention life).

We try to introduce these complications one by one. First, we can deal with the fact that defense spending is designed to reduce the probability of loss by evaluating its impact in terms of its effect on the expected value of loss. Keeping with the police protection model, and ignoring the possibility that the country can be destroyed, suppose that one dollar's worth of defense spending will reduce the probability that ten dollars' worth of resources will be stolen by 10 percent. Then the expected value of the defense spending is just one dollar—a ten-dollar gain times a 10 percent chance. Dealing with the fact that much of defense spending is on long-lived goods is also conceptually straightforward. Suppose that we can buy a piece of hardware that lasts for five years and that reduces the probability that ten dollars' worth of goods will be lost by 10 percent in each year. Then the expected value of the hardware is 10 percent of the present value of ten dollars a year for five years. Suppose that in this case the cost of the hardware is just equal to the expected present value of the losses that its deployment avoids. Then the entire cost of the hardware would be properly viewed as investment—consumption now is foregone in order to increase (expected) consumption in the future, and the present value of the future consumption that is increased, when evaluated at the interest rate, covers the cost of the asset that is acquired in the current period. It is in this sense that much of the 39 percent of defense spending classified as investment in Special Analysis D may be properly classified as investment, though obsolescence and depreciation costs should be deducted from the 39 percent to be more precise. Under these conditions, we would be purchasing the optimal amount of defense equipment; it would be earning the same rate of return, evaluated in terms of the expected effect on consumption, as private investment.

The fact that war is not just about property (or even perhaps very much about property) complicates the picture even more. The costs of engaging in war, much less nuclear war, are enormous, and the bulk of the costs are not consumption goods lost, but lives lost. To the extent that defense expenditures reduce the probability of war, the lessons of the simple model carry through—however the costs of war are evaluated, reducing the probability clearly has value, and in principle the value can be expressed as the cost of war times the amount the probability is reduced. Moreover, reductions in the probability of war have both investment and consumption components. The consumption component is obvious. Those who are alive now will bear the major costs of a war fought now. Their consumption will be reduced, in many cases to zero. The investment component is more difficult to ascertain, but is surely also real. The majority of members of this society would like this society to hold together, and grow, for generations now young or unborn.

And finally, we must consider the possibility of retaliation. To this point we assumed that increases in defense expenditures, whether for current services or long-lived equipment, increase safety. But suppose they lead the other side to respond—for the invaders to develop stronger wall-crushing implements. In such a scenario, rises in U.S. defense spending may actually be counterproductive; that is, they may require *more*—not less—expenditure on defense goods in the future to maintain some level of security. The importance of costly retaliatory measures on both sides cannot be discounted.

Given the current state of world weaponry, it is the prevention of war that has the great investment component, and to the extent that expenditures undertaken by the federal government reduce the probability of nuclear war, they should be seen in part as investment, although the calculation of rates of return seems beyond the conceptual framework of economics. On the other side, to the extent that current defense expenditures—including spending on weapons systems that are capital goods in the sense that they will last a long time—increase the probability of war, as suggested above, they are negative investment; they reduce future consumption possibilities at the cost of current consumption. Obviously, no government would undertake activities that were believed to have only negative payoffs, yet many experts in this area have argued persuasively that much of current defense expenditure in the United States is of precisely this form.[3]

Where does all of this leave us? On the basic consideration of whether defense spending should be fundamentally treated as investment or consumption, there is certainly a sense in which it is investment in the future security of America. Of course, one could make a similar argument about domestic spending for health or education. And with defense, the positive could easily turn to a negative when risk of retaliation is considered. In general, and certainly in this area, it is difficult to draw the line between consumption and investment from this point of view.

The more immediate practical question is not whether all defense spending is consumption or investment, but how the sharp increases since 1980 should be treated. If these rises in defense spending greatly increase national security, as some argue, our concern with the rises in the budget deficit that have taken place over the same period is overstated. Future generations should pay for some of their increased security. If the rises in defense spending are destabilizing and actually lower national security, as others argue, then our concern with the rises in the budget deficit is understated. For most of the analysis and tables in the book, we have adopted a fairly neutral posture: Increases in defense spending on hardware are assumed to have a net long-term security-increasing effect, but the effect decays rapidly. Hence our concern with the rises in the deficits depends mainly on the nonhardware components of defense spending. But we admit that, regarding defense-spending increases, our neutral assumption could be seriously in error on one side or the other.

Reducing Defense Spending

Regardless of the extent to which defense spending should be treated as investment or consumption, defense spending that does not reduce the probability of war or loss is simply wasted. Reducing the deficit by eliminating such spending is clearly in the national interest. In his recent discussion of the defense budget, William Kaufmann finds that a remarkable amount of currently planned defense spending is close to being wasted in this sense. He attributes the waste and redundancy to two causes: first, an overestimate of the extent to which the Soviet Union has been able to increase its military strength; and second, that the Department of Defense has engaged in poor management practices, leading to a good deal of wasteful duplication in the planned acquisition of weapons systems.

According to Kaufmann, by 1989 defense spending could be reduced by $46 billion dollars, relative to the CBO baseline we have been considering in this chapter. These savings could be effected "without weakening the nation's defense or altering basic strategy."[4] If this is so, the defense budget provides one possible source of budget reduction funds.

FEDERAL EMPLOYEES' RETIREMENT AND DISABILITY

There is widespread agreement, not necessarily shared by federal employees, that federal employees ought to have a pension system roughly in line with that of the private sector. Current federal pension plans are substantially more generous. Unlike most private pension plans, federal benefits are fully indexed for inflation. Unlike most private plans, employees can draw benefits well before age 62 if they have put in enough time on the job. There are also some undesirable incentives to retire from the military and continue to work, the so-called "double dipping" problem.

Because new federal employees are now covered by social security (effective 1984), it should now be technically possible to revise federal retirement and disability programs to be more in line with private plans. Although over the long run the budget savings may be considerable, by 1990 the savings from a typical plan will affect only those employees hired after 1984 and retiring before 1990, a very insignificant amount (about $1 billion, barely denting the baseline deficit). To get larger savings, the federal government would have to abrogate contractual commitments with its current employees, commitments similar to those made by General Motors or any other employer. And, like General Motors, the federal government cannot change the nature of those commitments radically without imperiling its ability to attract and retain quality employees. Thus, while there are grounds for believing that the retirement and disability provisions for federal employees are too generous, it is only by slowly changing the treatment of future retirees, and not by changing the treatment of those already retired, that budgetary savings can be effected.

MEANS-TESTED PROGRAMS

Means-tested programs are programs that are available to households and individuals only if their incomes are below some cutoff level. These are the programs that are loosely termed "welfare" in popular discussion, although it is worth pointing out here that the welfare program that receives the most attention, aid to families with dependent children (AFDC), is the fourth largest of the means-tested programs, and currently accounts for only $8 billion per year (projected to rise to $10 billion by 1990).

The set of means-tested programs discussed in this section has been cut considerably over the last few years, largely by making eligibility requirements more stringent. This has led to reduced support for the working poor, with the budgetary savings largely offset by the recession. With the improved performance in the economy, all of the means-tested programs except medicaid are projected to fall slightly as a percentage of GNP between now and 1990. Indeed, unless any concept of a "safety net" is to be abandoned, it is difficult to see how these programs can be reduced further, and there is considerable political agitation to increase them. Even if *all* of these programs were to be abolished tomorrow, they would reduce the 1990 deficit by less than one-third of its projected size. This is not where the money is. Moreover, it seems quite mean-spirited for a country as rich as the United States to take more out of the hide of the poor, when the share of the population in poverty status is already rising sharply.

Medicaid

Medicaid is designed to provide medical care for the poor. In most states, one is not eligible to receive medicaid unless one is a recipient of another means-tested program, usually AFDC or supplementary security income, which provides income to the low-income aged, blind, and permanently disabled. The reason that medicaid expenditures are projected to stay in constant real terms during the next five years, in contrast to the rest of means-tested programs, is that the costs of medical care will continue to rise (as with medicare), in this case balancing program reductions. Since 1981, eligibility and benefits under medicaid have been tightened considerably, and it has always been true that coverage varies a good deal by state. Many poor people are not covered even now. Unless the program is to be substantially changed in its purpose, the most promising route to reducing projected outlays would be by making systematic reforms in the way medicaid reimburses health-care providers. Short of these systematic and fundamental reforms, there seems little room to reduce the deficit by reducing medicaid outlays.

OTHER MANDATORY PROGRAMS

The major mandatory programs not yet discussed are veterans' benefits, farm price supports, and general revenue sharing. Of these, it would have seemed inconceivable until now that scheduled veterans' benefits would be reduced. Even if they are now more at risk because of budgetary exigencies, the total amount is projected at only $13 billion in 1990, a small amount relative to the size of the deficit.

General revenue sharing, although not very large ($5 billion in 1990), is a program with a tenuous justification. The program was begun at a time when the fiscal position of the federal government was strong relative to that of state and local governments—a time that plainly has passed. Basically, what revenue sharing does is give localities unrestricted grants to spend more or less as they see fit. The best available evidence indicates that revenue sharing has little effect on the volume or composition of local spending. Rather, it is a program that taxes people at the federal level and returns the money to localities which then use the bulk of the money to reduce taxes at the local level. There is a rationale for such a program to aid poor communities with low tax bases. But general revenue sharing is not heavily targeted on poor communities, and unless it can become better focused, the claim for generalized local tax relief is weak.

Whatever the ultimate desirability of this and other grant programs, we should also make one other point. Much of the interest in reducing government expenditures is in avoiding higher taxes. If most grants operate, as we suspect (and as plenty of evidence shows), to lower state and local taxes, cuts in grants will cause state and local taxes to rise. These cuts in grants may or may not be desirable; but we should understand that they do not reduce taxes—they only move them from one level of government to another.

Farm price supports have a number of purposes, and by and large accomplish none of them well. One of their stated purposes is to improve the incomes of small farmers. The way they are structured, however, the vast bulk of the payments go to large farmers with already high incomes. If the federal government has an interest in a welfare program aimed at the working farmer, price supports are a remarkably inefficient way to pursue that interest. According to a Brookings team, the 12 percent of farms with more than $100,000 in annual income account for more than two-thirds of the price-support payments made.

The other major purpose of price-support programs is to stabilize farm incomes, a sensible goal in light of the fact that farm prices fluctuate greatly from year to year. But if the goal is simply to stabilize incomes, the net long-term costs to the government should be quite low, income can be stabilized around its mean, with loans being advanced to farmers in years when income is low, and being repaid in years when it is high. When such a program stabilizes incomes around a high level, the program gives farmers an incentive to produce more output than is warranted at market prices. To avoid the unwanted accumulation of large stockpiles of agricultural commodities, the government must then resort to non-price restraints on production. The result is an expensive agricultural policy that performs neither of its intended functions well.

47

The CBO has estimated that a policy designed solely to stabilize commodity prices, but not to raise incomes on average, would save 60 percent of the currently forecast budget for price supports. In 1989, such savings would amount to $7.2 billion. This may be an overestimate of total savings from making the program change, however, because undoubtedly some sort of income maintenance program for low-income farmers would be retained. Still, the net savings could be substantial, and have the added advantage of increasing the competitiveness of U.S. agriculture.

DISCRETIONARY PROGRAMS

Nondefense discretionary programs comprise all other domestic activities of the federal government. Included here are the construction of roads and bridges, the subsidy to the post office, the operations of the national parks, the FBI, the judicial system, the collection of taxes, the imposition of customs duties, the maintenance and construction of canals and harbors, the air traffic control system, and the many regulatory activities of government. Also included are foreign aid, support for nondefense research and development, support for business and commerce and a number of nonentitlement programs that provide assistance to individuals (including various homeownership subsidies, veterans' hospitals, education and training programs, and low-income energy assistance). All of these programs together account for less than 20 percent of federal expenditures, and are not projected to grow in real terms over the next five years.

There is undoubtedly some room to cut many of these programs. Many outlays could be reduced by more active use of user fees to charge the direct beneficiaries of the programs for their costs, something of clear value in both equity and efficiency terms. One such example is the post office: It is not clear why junk mailers merit a public subsidy.

Many other programs work in the form of grants to state and local governments. As was pointed out earlier, often these grants do not raise state-local spending on public services—their intention—but instead merely allow for tax cuts at the state-local level. This makes them desirable programs to cut on efficiency grounds. But, as with general revenue sharing, we should be aware that if grants are cut, the most likely result is a rise in state and local taxes.

UNDISTRIBUTED OFFSETTING RECEIPTS

This category is included for completeness only, and is something of an illogical hodgepodge in the budget that provides very little promise as a means of reducing net outlays in any meaningful way. The largest item in the category (accounting for about 50 percent) is due to the way in which the federal government as employer is treated in the budget when contributions are made on behalf of employees retirement and disability programs. Such payments are counted as an outlay in the budgets of the individual agencies that make them, and their receipt by the treasury is counted as an undistributed offsetting receipt. In these cases, there is by definition no hope for reducing the deficit.

Most of the remaining offsetting receipts are derived from the sale or lease of federal lands, or from royalties paid on oil that is produced on the outer continental shelf. These are all cases where part of U.S. wealth is being used up now rather than later, and in which the government is able to derive some revenue from their use. In light of our discussion in earlier chapters, to reduce the deficit by accelerating the rate at which we permit resources to be used up is of no help in correcting the true economic costs of structural budget deficits. Using the resources represents one more element of the consumption binge that the deficit itself represents. Far from representing governmental saving, any revenue derived from this use is just an asset transfer that facilitates the present-day consumption. Although increases in offsetting receipts reduce the deficit as measured (in fact, they do not reduce the NIA deficit, which excludes asset transactions), they aggravate the consequences of the deficits.

THE GRACE COMMISSION
AND MANAGEMENT IMPROVEMENTS

For the most part, we have conveyed the disheartening message that the path to balanced budgets involves either radical change in what the government does or substantial increases in government revenue, the topic of the next chapter. At the same time, the report of the President's Private Sector Survey on Cost Control (the Grace Commission) concluded that management improvements could be undertaken that would yield $424 billion over a three-year period. Although reductions of this magnitude would not eliminate the deficit, they would cut it in half. Is the Grace Commission onto something that we are missing?

Unfortunately, analyses of the Commission's work are essentially unanimous on the point that the Grace Commission has dramatically overestimated possible budget savings. One reason is that most of the large saving comes in areas that represent policy changes, rather than simple management improvements in the efficiency of government operations. Second, in many cases, agencies more experienced in how the federal budget works than were the members of the Grace Commission (notably the CBO and the General Accounting Office) have found that the savings estimated by the Commission are far higher than the savings that would actually be realized if the Commission's proposals were adopted. The differences are striking: The CBO and GAO examined in detail a set of Grace Commission proposals that accounted for $298.4 billion of the $424 billion in savings referred to above. They found that implementation of all of those proposals in October of 1984 would lead to savings of only $97.9 billion over a three-year period, about one-third of the

Grace Commission estimate.[5] Although many of the Grace Commission's recommendations seem worthwhile, its overall message is misleading—the country faces much more difficult tradeoffs than the Grace report seems to indicate.

CONCLUSIONS: SAVINGS ON THE OUTLAY SIDE

It may seem strange that with more than $1378 billion in spending projected for 1990, we come to the conclusion that there is not much fat in the budget. There are certainly desirable cutbacks that can and should be made: The problem is that even if they are all made, a large budget deficit will still exist.

The main facts of the chapter can be summarized as follows:

1. Reducing the deficit through social security changes will have little budgetary effect unless tax rates are kept unchanged, which is difficult to do in the short run for political reasons, and in the long run for actuarial reasons.

2. Medicare outlays can be cut significantly only by radically changing the program or the nature of the market for medical care. There is an argument for reducing medicare's impact on the deficit by increasing revenues in order to pay for the program, but there is little room on the spending side.

3. Defense spending could perhaps be reduced by as much as $50 billion without affecting the U.S. defense posture. This is the best single opportunity for large savings. But even here any larger reductions would involve a change in U.S. strategy. The desirability of such a change is a matter of public policy, not budgeting.

4. Interest payments are an obligation of the government. They can be reduced by reducing other spending, or by raising revenues. The sooner the better.

5. The rest of the budget, consisting of means-tested programs and other activities of the government, has ceased to be a source of growth in the past five years or so. There are potential cutbacks here, but most are small potatoes, and many really represent local tax increases in disguise.

The problem is that most of the promising candidates for reduction have already been found in the past few years, and there is relatively little left to cut outside of the key areas of defense, social security, and interest payments. There is, of course, still fat left in the budget, but very little that can be cut out without a significant amount of political courage.

NOTES

[1] Previous chapters discussed the connection between public and private saving. This connection becomes particularly relevant for social security because the program can be viewed as almost a direct substitute for private savings. Although

the question is very complicated, if social security benefits were to fall and taxes were to be left unchanged, the private saving for retirement by present-day workers could rise. The empirical evidence in support of the proposition is weak—see Henry J. Aaron, *Economic Effects of Social Security*, The Brookings Institution, Washington, D.C., 1983. Moreover, as Aaron argues, if it were desired to raise national saving and investment, a far simpler way would be simply to run a budget surplus.

[2] See William W. Kaufmann, "Paying for National Security," in Alice M. Rivlin (ed.), *Economic Choices*, The Brookings Institution, Washington, D.C., 1984.

[3] See Freeman J. Dyson, *Weapons and Hope*, Harper and Row, New York, 1984, for an illuminating discussion of these issues, one that has concrete suggestions for changing the form, if not the magnitude, of defense spending in ways that might reduce the probability of war.

[4] See Kaufmann, "Paying for National Security."

[5] See the CBO and GAO, *Analysis of the Grace Commission Proposals for Cost Control*, United States Government Printing Office, Washington, D.C., February, 1984, pp. 7–9.

CHAPTER FIVE
TAXES

We have seen that reducing federal spending can at best eliminate about half of the deficit projected for 1990. Even that amount supposes some major program reductions and a sharp reduction in the growth of defense spending relative to what is currently projected. The inescapable conclusion is that in order to reduce the deficit to anything near zero in 1990, federal tax revenues must be increased by at least $100 billion in that year. To the extent that spending cuts fall short of what we have already discussed, the tax increases must be that much larger. Moreover, because the 1982 and 1984 tax changes have already made most of the reforms that might be considered easy (and some that were not), it is quite simply beyond possibility that the necessary revenues can be raised within the current tax structure without a large increase in tax rates.

There are two main alternatives:

1. A new tax source, such as a value-added tax or a national sales tax, could be introduced.
2. The current personal income tax, which is the major revenue source for the federal government, could be substantially reformed. In this case, by broadening the overall tax base to include much income that is currently exempt from tax, revenue could be increased and the overall schedule of tax rates could be lowered. People would, of course, be paying higher taxes, but the economic costs of taxes, which depend largely on the rates people pay on their incomes at the margin, could be reduced.

In this chapter we will consider both of these possibilities; we argue that the most equitable and efficient route to providing sources of increased revenue is major reform of personal and corporate income taxes.

Before going into the analysis, it is worth putting the problem in historical and comparative perspective. Assuming no major changes in tax structure, and assuming that state and local governments continue to raise the same share of GNP in revenues that they did in 1984, total government tax revenues in 1990 will be about 31.2 percent of GNP. This level is low in comparison with that of most other developed economies. For example, in 1981 Sweden's taxes were 59 percent of GNP, France's 46 percent, and Germany's 45 percent. Only Japan, of the major industrial countries, was below the United States at 29 percent. The projection for the United States share in 1990 is for levels somewhat higher than those of the 1960s and early 1970s, and somewhat lower than those of 1981 and 1982, when total tax collections reached 32.6 percent of GNP. If the entire deficit were to be made up through tax increases, the share of GNP accounted for by taxes would rise to about 36.5 percent in 1990, which would be a peacetime high for the United States, but which would still be lower than Sweden, France, and England. If budget cuts were to be used to reduce the deficit by as much as half, total government revenues required to balance the budget in 1990 (assuming that deficits would also be reduced along the way, thus reducing 1990 interest costs) would be about 33 percent of GNP, still above historical norms—but not by much. Such a figure would again be at the low end relative to other developed economies, suggesting that there does seem to be room for the aggregate U.S. tax burden to grow.

It is worth remembering that eliminating the measured deficit is not our ultimate objective here. The ultimate objective, and the reason we focus on taxes, is to raise, or prevent from falling, the share of national output devoted to capital formation. In this sense, there are better and worse ways of increasing taxes, and in this chapter we will develop criteria that might be used to evaluate alternative tax systems.

Finally, we note that there is nothing magic about a given level of public spending or taxes. The analyses of the first few chapters show that current taxpayers should be paying for their government spending. Chapter 4 shows that it is highly unlikely that this society will achieve that goal entirely by reducing spending. Indeed, it is possible that spending should be increased in some areas, and that some domains of public policy are sufficiently important that it would be better to continue spending, even at the cost of deficits, than to cut programs. This chapter, then, looks for ways in which those currently benefitting from the operations of the federal government can pay for what they get.

AN OVERVIEW

Table 5.1 and Fig. 5.1 show the major sources of federal revenue for selected years since 1970, along with the current-law CBO projections, to 1990. Table 5.1 also includes total state and local revenues (except intergovernmental grants).[1] The sum of federal and state and local revenues gives a measure of the total governmental tax burden.

A number of trends emerge from these data. First, the share of total revenue accounted for by the personal income tax rose through the 1970s, fell after the

TABLE 5.1 Composition of Actual and Projected Government Revenues, Selected Fiscal Years 1970–1990 (in billions of current dollars and as a percent of GNP indicated in parentheses)

	1970	1980	1985	1988	1990
Individual Income Taxes	90	244	333	432	515
	(9.3)	(9.5)	(8.6)	(8.9)	(9.2)
Corporate Income Taxes	33	65	63	96	107
	(3.4)	(2.5)	(1.6)	(2.0)	(1.9)
Social Insurance Taxes	44	158	266	333	389
	(4.6)	(6.1)	(6.9)	(6.9)	(6.9)
Excise Taxes	16	24	38	34	34
	(1.6)	(0.9)	(1.0)	(0.7)	(0.7)
Estate and Gift Taxes	4	6	6	5	5
	(0.4)	(0.2)	(0.1)	(0.1)	(0.1)
Customs Duties	2	7	12	15	16
	(0.3)	(0.3)	(0.3)	(0.3)	(0.3)
Miscellaneous Receipts	3	13	18	19	21
	(0.4)	(0.5)	(0.5)	(0.4)	(0.4)
Total Federal Revenues	193	517	735	934	1088
	(19.9)	(20.1)	(19.1)	(19.3)	(19.4)
State and Local Own-Source Revenues	109	299	455	570	662
	(11.1)	(11.5)	(11.8)	(11.8)	(11.8)
Total Government Revenues	302	816	1190	1504	1750
	(31.0)	(31.6)	(30.9)	(31.1)	(31.2)

Note: Details may not add to totals because of rounding.

Source: Federal revenue and GNP projections for 1985, 1988, and 1990 are from Congressional Budget Office, *The Economic and Budget Outlook: Fiscal Years 1986–1990,* February, 1985, Table II-9; data for 1970 and 1980 federal revenue and GNP are from Tables E-3 and E-4. State and local data for 1970 and 1980 are from *The Economic Report of the President, February, 1985.* Table B-77. Projections for state and local revenue for 1985, 1988, and 1990 assume the 1984 share of GNP.

1981 tax act, and is slowly rising again. Second, the sum of personal income taxes and social insurance taxes (the earmarked taxes used to finance the social insurance programs discussed in Chapter 4) has been rising as a percentage of GNP. These are the taxes that are probably most noticed by taxpayers—they come right out of the paycheck. Third, although corporate income taxes had been declining in importance (if slowly) throughout the 1970s, their importance was radically reduced by the 1981 tax act. Fourth, the personal income tax, social insurance taxes, and the corporate income tax are the only significant sources of federal revenue. The rest, by federal budget standards, is just nickels and dimes.

As was pointed out in Chapter 4, social insurance taxes are earmarked for particular programs. Because these funds cannot accumulate assets indefinitely, program benefits cannot be cut without their taxes being cut as well. Nor can taxes be raised without program benefits being raised. The one exception here is medicare, where the trust fund is already projected to run continuing deficits, and where taxes or benefits need to be readjusted to prevent continuing decumulation. Apart

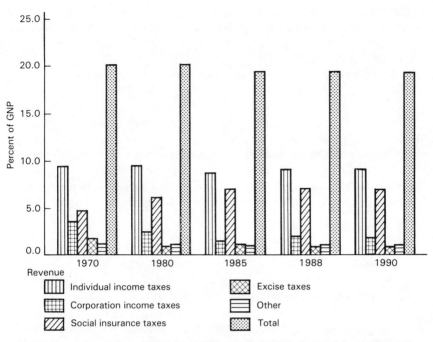

FIGURE 5.1 Composition of Actual and Projected Federal Revenues, Selected Fiscal Years, as a Percent of GNP.

from this problem, the potential for social insurance taxes to have much impact on the deficit is very limited, leaving the personal income tax and the corporate income tax as the current sources of federal revenue that bear some examination.

THE PERSONAL INCOME TAX

By far the most important federal tax, the personal income tax is a logical candidate to be used to increase revenues. An increase in tax rates would be easy to administer, and given that everyone has a good deal of experience with the tax, such an increase would be well understood. Unfortunately, this course of action is unattractive both politically and economically. It is unattractive politically because the personal income tax is widely viewed to be full of loopholes and unfair. It is unattractive economically for similar reasons—the "loopholes," or types of income that are subject to no or low tax, lead to economic inefficiency of two types:

1. Many loopholes merely serve to stimulate expenditure on items that serve no particular public purpose—they distort the composition of GNP toward things that receive favorable treatment and away from everything else.
2. The fact that the tax base is reduced by excessive numbers of deductions and exemptions means that in order to raise a given amount of revenue, tax rates

55

must be higher than they would otherwise be. This leads to distortions in individuals' choices about hours of work, saving versus consumption, and so on. Any tax system will cause such inefficiencies, but the magnitude of the cost increases roughly as the square of the tax rate, implying that loopholes that in themselves cause little problem may cause serious problems by requiring higher marginal tax rates.[2]

Given that the current system is viewed as being both unfair and inefficient, and that raising the tax rates would only increase these difficulties, it would seem to be far more promising to revise the current system so as to broaden the tax base (remove loopholes) and permit lower tax rates. There would then be room to have tax rates high enough to reduce the deficit but perhaps lower than current rates on most sources of income. A number of tax reform proposals of this type have been advanced:

1. "Flat" tax proposals, which would eliminate most deductions from taxable income and tax the remainder at a uniform rate. Although these would do the job, it is clear that their impact would be to shift the tax burden to low- and middle-income people. There is no way mathematically for a perfectly flat-rate income tax to raise the current level of revenue or more without increasing taxes on middle-income households relative to high-income households.[3]

2. The current progressivity of the tax structure (the feature whereby the fraction of income paid in tax rises as income rises) could be retained, at lower tax rates, if the tax base were broadened—similarly to the flat tax proposals—but a set of tax rates that rose with income were imposed on the new, broader base. Although such proposals are often misnamed "modified flat tax" or "progressive flat tax," they are in fact simply broadly based progressive income taxes (PIT), and would represent a return to a simpler tax structure than the one that has evolved.

   Two of the leading candidates here, both proposed by ex-sports heroes who have become politicians, are the "Fair" tax of Senator Bill Bradley and Representative Richard Gephardt, and the "Fast" tax of Representative Jack Kemp and Senator Bob Kasten. (Why is it that all tax plans are named by four letter words beginning with F?) A third, as yet without formal political status, was devised by the Treasury Department in November, 1984. None of the existing modified flat tax proposals raise new revenue; but they could easily be modified to do that.[4]

3. The personal income tax could be replaced by a personal expenditure tax (PET), also at progressive rates. The difference between the two taxes is wholly in their treatment of income from capital, precisely the area that has the greatest problems (and biggest loopholes) in the current income tax.

Although the pure flat tax proposals are by far the simplest of the three to administer, their impact on the income distribution, if enough revenue is to be raised, is to help the rich get richer at the expense of most everyone else.[5] If this impact is to be avoided, the choice is between the PET and the PIT. For reasons that will become apparent later, we tend to favor the PET and conduct most of the discussion using it as a basis. But the differences between a PET and a PIT with a much broader base are not terribly large, and many of our comments refer to base-broadened income taxes as well. We conclude by discussing some desirable reforms that make sense, either in the context of a PET or a PIT.

A PERSONAL EXPENDITURE TAX[6]

The basic idea of an expenditure tax is very simple—it taxes consumption expenditures but not income. The natural way to assess the tax would be to retain the present administrative machinery for collecting personal income taxes, with one crucial difference: Taxpayers would be allowed to deduct their saving from the tax base, but would be taxed on their dissaving. Although the tax base would be changed, all desirable features of the personal income tax could be retained. In particular, the PET as we envision it would be progressive, taxing upper-income households at higher average rates, and it would have a personal exemption, just like the current income tax. Moreover, although many current "charitable" deductions should probably be repealed (either from the PET or the income tax), the charitable deduction provision could still be retained, allowing the PET to be used as a way of encouraging private eleemosynary activity.

Implementation of the PET in its simplest form is straightforward. As is the case now, taxpayers would file returns in which they would report their annual income. Their tax base would be equal to their income less any saving plus any withdrawals from savings. In order to measure the latter two amounts, banks, stockbrokers, insurance companies, and other institutions would establish qualified accounts—much like current individual retirement accounts (IRAs). Payments into qualified accounts would be deducted from the tax base, and withdrawals from such accounts, both principal amounts and returns to capital, would be added to the tax base. By way of example, if a taxpayer earns $30,000, buys $3000 worth of stock, puts $1200 into a savings account, receives $300 interest from a savings account, and sells $1000 worth of bonds, she would have a tax base of $27,100; her total receipts would be $31,300, and her gross saving would be $4200. The tax base, personal expenditure, is simply receipts minus saving. Alternatively, the tax base can be viewed as income ($30,300) less net saving ($3200). Note that if the taxpayer left the $300 in savings-account interest in the account, that amount would have been treated as saving (or not included in receipts), giving a tax base of $26,800.

Borrowing under a PET is treated as expenditure; repayments are treated as saving. Thus if a taxpayer borrows $4000 in a year, she will add that amount to her tax base. Repayments of both principal and interest would be deductible. Note that this is precisely symmetrical to the treatment of borrowing and lending discussed earlier. In all cases, net saving and repayment of old loans is deductible from the tax base while new borrowing (negative net saving) is added to the tax base.

Record-keeping requirements under the PET would be only slightly more extensive than those under a personal income tax. Financial institutions (broadly defined to include stockbrokers and the like) would have to keep track of deposits and withdrawals, and report the net difference for each taxpayer every year. Under current practice, although deposits and withdrawals are not reported to the IRS, such records are kept by brokers and banks. Implementation of the PET would require that this information be given to taxpayers and to the IRS in each year, so that each taxpayer could report net deposits into qualified accounts. Note that it is very much in the interest of taxpayers to use qualified accounts for their saving; if they do not do so, they do not qualify for the deduction. Having put money into qualified accounts when saved, the taxpayer will have difficulty hiding receipts when withdrawals are made, because the institutions at which the accounts are kept will be required to report all withdrawals to the IRS.[7]

TAXATION OF CAPITAL INCOME

One major advantage of the PET over most types of income taxes is that the PET removes essentially all of the current difficulties involved in the taxation of income from capital and savings. Current treatment of capital income is an unholy mess. Taxpayers who keep ordinary savings accounts are taxed on their interest income in every year. They receive a real rate of return equal to $r(1-t) - p$ where r is the interest rate, t is the taxpayer's marginal income tax rate, and p is the rate of inflation. Taxpayers with IRAs or holding state and local bonds, on the other hand, receive consumption tax treatment. Their real rate of return is $r - p$ (the interest rate minus the inflation rate).

Capital gains are treated in still a different way under an income tax. The fact that gains are taxed only upon realization is of great value to taxpayers—they accumulate returns tax free, and if the gains are postponed long enough, the effective tax rate approaches zero. Indeed, when capital gains are made part of a bequest, the tax rate is zero, because the recipient of the bequest never has to pay taxes on the gain that accumulated during the lifetime of the donor. On the other hand, inflation raises the effective tax rate on capital gains because whatever tax is imposed is imposed on the increase in an asset's nominal value since the time it was purchased. The exemption of 60 percent (increased from 50 percent in 1978) of long-term gains from taxation may be thought of as an adjustment for the effect of inflation, but the adjustment is at best imperfect, and the correct adjustment would change with the rate of inflation and the time that the asset was purchased—causing insurmountable problems of tax administration. Indeed, the only proper treatment of capital gains in an income tax system is to tax the real (inflation-adjusted) accrued gains every year—causing even more insurmountable administrative *and* political problems, because people have to hand over income they have not yet realized.

Investment in consumer durables and housing is taxed in still a different way. Again the return from the asset—now an "imputed" return, basically reflecting the fact that owners do not have to pay rent—is nontaxable. Property taxes (which can be viewed as a user fee for public services provided by the locality) can be deducted; other explicit user fees cannot, and capital gains on homes are taxed very lightly, quite often not at all.

The existence of tax-free and tax-preferred forms of saving in conjunction with the deductibility of interest payments from individual tax bases leads to a phenomenon called *tax arbitrage* that seriously compromises the integrity of the income tax. Currently, it is possible for taxpayers to take out loans or sell taxable assets to purchase tax-exempt assets.[8] A taxpayer in a 50-percent bracket can borrow money (or sell taxable assets) at 14 percent and invest in an exempt IRA at 10 percent, realizing a rate of return of 3 percent after tax without doing any saving at all. The after-tax cost of the borrowing (or asset sale) is only 7 percent; the entire 10 percent return is untaxed. Although the amount that can be invested in an IRA is limited, the amounts that can be invested in tax-exempt municipal bonds or that can take advantage of very lightly taxed homes and assets on which capital gains are earned are not limited.

Although some of these tax preferences on the asset side were introduced into the tax code to stimulate saving, the fact that the interest deduction is not limited provides taxpayers with an opportunity to generate returns solely by manipulating their assets so as to take advantage of the tax rules, without doing any new saving at all. The main impact on overall national saving and investment is negative: Because revenue is lost to the treasury, deficits are larger and capital formation is lower than would otherwise be the case. Tax arbitrage possibilities work against the offsetting rise in private saving. (We mentioned this in our earlier chapters.) Ironically, then, measures introduced to stimulate personal saving ultimately reduce total economy-wide saving and capital formation.

Even more significant problems arise in connection with the taxation of physical assets. Ideally, an income tax would tax real returns from physical assets. Thus, the tax base should be equal to the income generated by the asset less the value of physical depreciation on the asset. Implementation of this standard requires that depreciation be accurately measured, year by year, and deducted from the tax base. When there is no inflation, it is at least imaginable that such treatment could be approximated. The Treasury Department could make estimates, asset type by asset type, of physical depreciation, and apply those estimates to assets held by taxpayers (either directly or through stock held in businesses). When there is inflation, things become much more complicated, because the value of the asset used to calculate depreciation should be adjusted for the general increase in prices. If the basis for depreciation is not indexed, the real value of depreciation deductions will be eroded by inflation, leading to a tax base that is larger than true income from the asset.

Indexing of depreciation allowances has never been practiced in the United States, although it was proposed in the Treasury's 1984 tax plan. Until now, Congress has responded to changing rates of inflation by allowing holders of physical assets to deduct depreciation on an accelerated schedule. During the 1970s, the connection between estimates of actual physical depreciation and the rate at which the Treasury permits depreciation deductions was made ever more tenuous, culminating in the Accelerated Cost Recovery System (ACRS) in 1981, under which there is essentially no relationship between actual depreciation and depreciation allowable for tax purposes. The simultaneous impact of ACRS and the investment tax credit, available only for equipment, according to Council of Economic Advisers' estimates, has led to before-tax rates of return on various types of physical assets that range from more than 6 percent on industrial structures to less than 3 percent on equipment.[9] When one considers specific assets (rather than broad classes), the variation is much larger. What this implies is that the tax system leads to a pattern of investment that is inefficient: Capital could be reallocated from its less productive uses to its more productive uses to give a significant rise in output at no long-run cost. If the tax system were neutral, the United States would have more structures, less equipment, and greater GNP at zero marginal resource cost.[10]

This discussion should make it clear that high on the agenda for tax reform must be improvement of the taxation of capital income. The major elements of such reform—uniform treatment of assets, elimination of major opportunities for tax arbitrage, and rendering the system proof against distortions caused by inflation—are possible under either a PET or a reformed PIT. In order to effect such reforms under a PIT, it is essential to measure accurately the physical depreciation of assets (because only depreciation can be deducted under an income tax), to index the basis for depreciation, to eliminate preferential treatment of capital gains, and to index the basis for capital gains computation as well. Further, in order to eliminate tax arbitrage, a PIT would require rules that limit taxpayers' interest deductions to their taxable investment incomes, perhaps with a little leeway.

Although configuration of PIT to achieve the goals mentioned here is not impossible, it is also not straightforward. Indexing of depreciation and capital gains requires choosing an appropriate index. Measurement of actual depreciation is cumbersome, so at best general guidelines would have to be used, although the guidelines could be made much closer to actual behavior than those currently in force. Also, rules that limited interest deductions would cause some difficulties in practice. Both the Treasury plan and the Bradley–Gephardt proposal would move the PIT in the directions suggested here, although Bradley–Gephardt would not index depreciation and capital gains.

Under the PET, the reform proposed here can be effected without the need for special rules and guidelines. All assets, both financial and physical, would receive treatment that is the equivalent of "expensing." The entire cost of the asset would be deducted when the asset was acquired, and all proceeds from the asset, including resale, would be taxed as they were realized. Inflation would not cause any problems for the taxation of capital income, because there are no deductions that need indexing. Real after-tax income from capital will be independent of inflation, provided that inflation does not change the taxpayer's tax bracket. The problem of bracket creep is identical under both the progressive PET and the PIT; if desired, this problem can be corrected by indexing the personal exemption and tax brackets.

It is worth noting that the way in which the PET accomplishes rational and inflation-proof taxation of capital income is by failing to tax the normal returns to new capital at all. For both physical and financial assets, the treatment just outlined yields a tax base with a present value equal to the purchase price of the asset. Plainly, if the tax base is just equal to the purchase price and the initial purchase is deductible, an asset that earns a normal rate of return (the interest rate used to calculate the present value) is exempt from tax. If there are unusually large returns, they are added to the tax base when the returns are realized. If the returns are unusually small, the tax base is reduced by the difference between the realized returns and normal returns.

Desirable as all this is on efficiency grounds, it may be argued that on equity grounds, normal returns to capital should be included in the tax base, as they would be under the PIT. At present, capital income taxation is such a mess that only the particularly naive could believe that it serves any equity goal at all. Under a PET, capital income, like all other income, is taxed when it is used, and the tax rate depends on the taxpayer's consumption, not the form of investment. This, we would argue, is an improvement—on both efficiency and equity grounds—over current practice.

BASE BROADENING AND RATE REDUCTION

The PET uses consumption as its tax base: the PIT uses income. In an economy with net saving, the tax base of an income tax is potentially larger than that of the PET, suggesting that a disadvantage of the PET is that it would require higher average tax rates in order to raise a given revenue. Although this is true in principle, it is not true when a PET is compared either to the present income tax or to the major reform proposals for the PIT now under consideration. This is because the current U.S. income tax is so far from a pure income tax that even attempts to reform it generate less than the ideal tax base. As we have noted, much of capital income is already exempt, there are many other loopholes, and the problem of tax arbitrage further reduces the tax base. In a recent paper, Henry Aaron and Harvey Galper estimate that a PET—much along the lines of the one discussed here—would have a considerably larger tax base than the current income tax, and thus could raise sufficient revenue to meet the goals outlined at the beginning of this chapter, with larger personal exemptions and lower marginal tax rates than are obtained under the current income tax.[11]

PROBLEMS WITH THE MAJOR TAX REFORM

Movement to either the PET or a comprehensively based PIT would be something of a radical change, and there will be transition difficulties associated with the move. Further, if a PET were adopted, there would be some problems of tax administration, notably the treatment of housing and consumer durables, that would take considerable work to get right. Many lawyers and economists have tried to work out these problems, and they do seem to be surmountable. There is one major problem, however, that must be dealt with if the PET is to be viewed as superior to a broadly based income tax—that of estate and gift taxation.

Without estate and gift taxation, the expenditure tax contains a serious loophole. It would be possible for taxpayers to accumulate wealth by saving throughout their lifetime and then passing their wealth along to heirs, with no one paying any tax at all. The same is now possible under the income tax, because capital gains never have to be realized and may be included as part of bequests, at which point the gain during the lifetime of the donor becomes exempt from tax.[12] Though present PIT plans should have focused on this loophole, too, they have not. Under a PET, the obvious solution would be to treat bequests as a form of consumption, and require the estate to pay tax on bequests (perhaps after some small exemption) at the applicable rate on personal expenditure.[13] This provision would also have the nice feature that the lifetime tax base for any taxpayer would be just equal to lifetime income (consumption plus accumulated wealth must just equal income over any accounting period).

THE CORPORATE INCOME TAX

Economists have long decried the corporate income tax, in part because it is almost impossible to figure out who really pays it, and in part because dividends are taxed twice, once at the corporate level and once at the personal level, to the detriment of capital formation and economic efficiency. Under either a PET or a PIT, some sort of direct business taxation is necessary, because without it there would be the possibility that resources could be accumulated in corporate form, and that business organizations could be used to escape all personal taxes. For example, one could incorporate, run all of one's receipts and expenditures through the corporation, and never pay tax. The lack of a corporate tax would also make it impossible to tax foreign owners of U.S. business, a group that is growing rapidly because of the open economy capital flows. (We discussed this in Chapter 2.) To close these loopholes, it seems that in conjunction with either a PET or a reformed PIT, the United States should adopt a system of business taxation similar to the one first proposed by E. Cary Brown back in 1948.[14]

The idea behind the Brown tax was to find a way to tax pure economic rent, because a tax on pure rent is nondistorting. The approach is to levy a tax in which all business expenses other than pure rent would be deductible, and all receipts would be taxable—in short, an expenditure tax on corporations. A tax of this type would have a present value of receipts just equal to zero under conditions of perfect competition without pure rents (total receipts would just equal total expenses when the zero profit condition of perfect competition applied). Thus, any revenue raised would be attributable to monopoly profits or other types of economic rent, and would be nondistorting.

The correct treatment of physical assets under such a tax is to permit deduction for the purchase price and to include all receipts as taxable cash flow. If an asset is financed by borrowing, the value of the loan is counted as a receipt, and interest and repayments are deductible. Compared with the present cumbersome corporate tax, this treatment involves immediate expensing of physical investments financed internally or by the sale of stock, with no subsequent depreciation (and inflation adjustment problems). If assets are financed by loans, there is no expensing but there is deduction of interest and principal repayments. Alternatively, the loan-financed asset could also be expensed, but then the interest and principal repayments would not be deductible.

In all cases, for an asset with the same (normal) rate of return as the interest rate, the present value of the tax liability would be zero. There would be positive tax liability only if the asset earned an above-normal rate of return, implying a return to some factor that received economic rent. Recall that investors would be allowed to deduct loans they made or stock that they purchased, and that under the PET the present value of tax liability on income from these sources would also be zero. Because zero plus zero is zero, there would be no problem of double taxation (as there is under the current corporate income tax) for assets earning normal rates of return. On assets earning higher returns, there would be double taxation, but there would be no distortion. On assets earning lower returns, the government would participate with both the business and the taxpayer in sharing the losses.[15] In order to assure that corporate organization was not used to avoid personal taxes, the corporate tax rate could also be set at the top personal rate.[16]

The corporate income tax could also be reformed along the lines of the Treasury plan or the Bradley-Gephardt proposal. Both of these would complement their reforms of the PIT by replacing the 1981 depreciation reforms with guidelines approximating true economic depreciation and lowering the corporate rate (to 30 percent for Bradley-Gephardt, and 33 percent for Treasury). With true economic depreciation, the corporate tax would once again become a tax on corporate income, rather than a tax at widely different rates on different types of corporate income. Either reform plan would be as easy to administer or lead to as little economic distortion as the Brown tax.

HALFWAY HOUSES

Either a pure income tax (with an associated corporate income tax that measured capital income accurately) or a pure expenditure tax would greatly enhance the ability of the federal government to increase tax revenues while improving the efficiency of the economy. For the reasons discussed in the last section, we would prefer the pure PET, but many of the PIT plans also represent a major improvement over the current system. However, it seems unlikely that a pure form of either tax will be adopted. Therefore, we also consider a number of reforms that would improve the tax system whether or not the basic tax is an income tax or an expenditure tax. Because many of the reforms we consider here are also features of the various reform proposals currently under discussion, we also use this section to comment on those proposals. Those proposals, like the more sweeping reforms we have already discussed, all involve broadening the tax base by eliminating tax expenditures of various kinds. Further, although the Bradley–Gephardt proposal retains a number of tax expenditures, the effect of these are curtailed in a way that tends to enhance progressivity and reduce revenue losses to the treasury. Under the Bradley–Gephardt proposal, deductions would all be converted to tax credits at the lowest marginal rate. Thus, even a taxpayer in the highest bracket would receive a deduction only at the rate applicable to taxpayers in the lowest bracket.

Deductibility of Interest

As long as there are tax-free forms of investment, the deductibility of interest payments provides taxpayers with the opportunity to engage in tax arbitrage. The biggest such opportunity, owner-occupied housing, is probably politically untouchable. But deductibility of mortgage interest could be limited to the household's principal residence (as it is under both Bradley–Gephardt and the Treasury proposal), and interest deductions for other borrowing could be limited to the amount of taxable investment income. Again, both Bradley–Gephardt and the Treasury proposal would implement such limitations, although the Treasury would allow up to $5000 a year of deductible interest in excess of investment income. Limitations of this kind would go a long way toward removing the problems that exist when there are PET-like features (such as IRAs and tax-free bonds) in an income tax system. They also make the saving subsidies raise private saving, which is their point in the first place. Thus they should be part of any reform of the income tax.

Deductibility of State and Local Taxes

In general, the deductibility of state and local taxes is difficult to rationalize on economic grounds. The bulk of such deductions is taken by high-income tax payers, thus reducing the progressivity of the federal tax system. On the argument that state and local taxes are really user fees for government services, they should be treated the same way as direct user fees, and considered a part of taxable income. The Treasury plan provides for just such treatment; Bradley–Gephardt would still allow the deduction (but only at the lowest marginal tax rate) of state and local income and property taxes.

Depreciation Reform

If the United States is to have an income tax, capital income must be measured more accurately. This requires that depreciation allowances be roughly equivalent to actual depreciation, and that such allowances be adjusted for inflation. Both major PIT proposals would repeal special depreciation provisions, but only the Treasury plan would also index depreciation allowances for inflation. Alternatively, it would be possible to move toward PET treatment of capital income by simply allowing all investment spending to be deducted at the time it is incurred provided that interest payments are made nondeductible.

Capital Gains

Under a PET, capital gains are nontaxable and pose no problem. Under a PIT, the basis for capital gains should be indexed (so that taxpayers do not pay tax on gains that arise from inflation alone), but the special treatment of such gains (currently 60 percent of long-term gains are deducted from income) should be eliminated. Both Treasury and Bradley-Gephardt would treat capital gains as ordinary income, but only Treasury would go the extra (and necessary) step of indexing them.

Estate and Gift Taxes

Under a PET-based system, bequests and gifts should be treated as consumption, and be taxed at the PET rates. If this is not done, there is great potential for amassing untaxed fortunes across generations. In the present income tax, the great loophole is the fact that capital gains are not taxed when they are parts of estates and gifts. If this loophole were closed, the logic of income taxation would not dictate reform of estate and gift taxation, although concern with the power inherent in great wealth provides an alternative argument for reform of the current system, which has been described as a "voluntary" tax by expert commentators.

When all is said and done, the essential task is to broaden the tax base, either along the lines of a PET or a PIT. Most of the proposals we have discussed here were raised in the context of a reformed PIT, and are clearly desirable there. To move to a PET, all that needs to be done is to substitute expensing for properly measured depreciation, give capital gains the same treatment as all capital income under the PET, and treat estates and gifts as personal expenditure. If the PIT is adopted, the ideas given here suggest that the Treasury plan is somewhat preferable to Bradley-Gephardt overall. On the other hand, if we recognize that there will probably be a number of "loopholes" in any tax system, the Bradley-Gephardt proposal that deductions should be of equal value (that of the lowest tax rate) for high- and low-income taxpayers alike is a promising middle ground.

NEW REVENUE SOURCES

Two possible sources of revenue have received a good deal of recent attention—a national sales tax, and, what is economically similar, a value-added tax (VAT). A national sales tax requires little explanation: Retailers simply add the percentage markup on their sales (as is now done in most states), with perhaps a mechanism for rebating sales taxes on goods resold over and over to avoid excessive taxation of them. Under a VAT, businesses would pay tax on the difference between the amount that they paid for goods and the amount that they sold the goods for. Thus, the tax base for a retailer would be his markup on sales; the tax base for a manufacturer of nails would be the difference between the cost of wire and the selling price of nails made from the wire. At each stage of production, the tax on prior stages would generally be included in the good's price, so the overall effect of a VAT would be very much like that of a sales tax.

There is widespread experience with the VAT in Europe, and sales tax administration is now practiced by almost all states in the United States, so either tax would be relatively easy to administer. There could be some serious problems in state–federal coordination where some goods were exempt from sales taxes at one level of government but not at the other, but there is no reason why the federal government could not simply impose its sales tax or VAT and let the states coordinate with it as they wish. Moreover, either tax could raise a good deal of revenue at relatively low rates. Indeed, each percentage point of a relatively broadly based value-added or sales tax would raise about $12 billion.[17] The problem with either of these options is that unless certain goods are exempted (reducing the base, increasing the rate, and adding distortions), or some offset is made in the income tax, a VAT or a sales tax will be regressive in its impact, even more so than a flat-rate income tax with a personal exemption. A second problem is that the short-run impact of either tax is likely to raise retail prices, and, if not adjusted for in cost-of-living escalators, be inflationary. A third problem is one that is often raised by fiscal conservatives. Once the administrative structure for a national tax of this kind is in place, it becomes much easier to increase federal revenues than is currently the case. Indeed, the European experience with the VAT is that although it was intended to replace existing taxes, it generally increased total governmental revenue.[18]

CONCLUSION

Elimination of the deficit will require a tax increase that amounts to more than $100 billion in 1990. The figure is much higher if spending is not cut or the tax increase does not begin to take effect well before 1990. In the latter case, the reason is because deficits run before 1990 will require higher interest payments then and thereafter. Such a tax increase is not feasible without substantial reform of the existing structure or imposition of a new tax. A PET levied at lower rates than the current income tax could raise the needed revenue, enhance economic efficiency, and simplify the lives of the taxpaying public. A broadened personal income tax, similar to one of the many plans now (in early 1985) being discussed in Washington, could have the same effect, but would leave intact a number of difficulties associated with the taxation of capital income and the behavior of the tax system at varying rates of inflation. Even so, a broadened personal income tax would be vastly superior to the current system: More revenue could be raised at lower marginal tax rates, implying some progress on the deficit problem and an improvement in overall economic efficiency. Moreover, a broadened personal income tax could be every bit as progressive as the current system, even though everyone would be paying substantially lower marginal tax rates. A value-added or national sales tax could also raise revenues and help whittle the deficit, but it would be relatively regressive. There is no choice but to adopt one of these alternatives if deficits are to disappear by the end of the decade.

NOTES

[1] Very often when people want to show how large government has become in the United States, they add federal, state, and local expenditures. Because some federal expenditures are grants to state and local governments which could either finance some of their expenditures or cause state and local tax reductions, this way of counting contains a potential bias. We have counted on the tax side, explicitly omitting grants, to avoid this source of contamination.

[2] For those with some training in microeconomics, the reason is as follows. Taxes can be thought of as shifting up the supply curve for some activity roughly in proportion to the tax rate. This introduces the famous deadweight loss triangle, the measure of the efficiency cost of the distortion. The area of this triangle is one-half times its height (proportional to the tax rate) times its base (proportional to the tax rate times the demand sensitivity).

[3] See Joseph J. Minarik, "The Future of the Individual Income Tax," *National Tax Journal,* Vol. 35, September, 1982, pp. 231–242.

[4] For discussions of these and other proposals, see Joseph A. Pechman (ed.), *A Citizen's Guide to the New Tax Reforms,* Rownan and Allenheed, 1985. For the Treasury plan in full detail, see U.S. Treasury, *Tax Reform for Families, Simplicity, and Economic Growth,* U.S. Department of Treasury, New York, 1984.

[5] See Minarik, "The Future of the Individual Income Tax." But we admit that this reservation is a subjective one. For those who want to pursue the possibility, we commend Robert E. Hall and Alvin Rabushka, *Low Tax, Simple Tax, Flat Tax,* McGraw-Hill, 1982, for a stirring argument on behalf of a flat-rate expenditure tax.

[6] Much of the material from this section is taken from the authors' "The Expenditure Tax: Has the Idea's Time Finally Come?" in Joseph A. Pechman et al., *Tax Policy: New Directions and Possibilities,* Center for National Policy, Washington, D.C., 1985.

[7] Individual borrowers could evade taxes by borrowing from friends and relatives who do not administer qualified accounts. However, it would not be in the interest of lenders to engage in such transactions, because they would not be able to deduct the amounts loaned from their tax bases. In general, the IRS would have to require that individual lenders seeking to deduct loans from their tax bases report the identification number of the taxpayer receiving the loan. Similarly, borrowers repaying such loans and deducting the repayments would have to identify the creditor. In all cases, it is in the interest of one of the parties to report the transaction, reinforcing an essential component of an effective personal tax system—self-reporting.

[8] Technically, borrowing in order to make tax-exempt investments is illegal, but as long as there is no restriction on the amount of interest payments that a taxpayer can deduct, it is easy to circumvent this provision.

[9] *The Economic Report of the President,* February, 1982, p. 123.

[10] Jane G. Gravelle, in "Capital Income Taxation and Efficiency in the Allocation of Investment," *National Tax Journal,* vol. 36, September, 1983, pp. 297–306, estimates that current tax-induced misallocations of capital amount to completely wasting about 2.5 percent of the capital stock (Tables 4 and 5), or 0.7 percent of GNP (p. 304). Don Fullerton and many co-authors (see, for example, Fullerton, John B. Shoven, and John Whalley, "Replacing the U.S. Income Tax with a Progressive Consumption Tax," *Journal of Public Economics,* vol. 20, February, 1983, pp. 3–23) also derive estimates of efficiency gains from consump-

tion taxation and of efficiency losses from current treatment. Because Fullerton's models require budget balance, they are not directly applicable here.

[11] Henry J. Aaron and Harvey Galper, "Reforming the Tax System," in Alice M. Rivlin (ed.), *Economic Choices*. The Brookings Institution, Washington, D.C., 1984. Aaron and Galper estimate that a personal expenditure exemption of $5000 for individuals, $8250 for couples, and $1500 for additional dependents coupled with marginal tax rates of 6 percent on the first $10,000 of taxable expenditure, 24 percent on the next $30,000, and 38 percent on all taxable expenditure over $40,000 would provide sufficient revenue to eliminate much of the deficit. All of these rates are lower than current rates; the tax liabilities of persons with low incomes are also much lower than at present.

[12] This problem was addressed by the 1978 tax law, but the provision was never implemented and was repealed in 1981.

[13] It is possible that during some transition period, given the fact that many individuals who would be leaving bequests in the relatively near future earned their income under an income tax and would be doubly taxed if their wealth were to be taxed as consumption, the tax on bequests could be levied at some transitional rate lower than the full expenditure tax rate. Indeed, such treatment could be applied to all consumption of taxpayers older than a particular age, with the rate rising to the full PET rate over a period of years. Although such a transition would be messy from an administrative standpoint and may not be warranted in light of the fact that the beneficiaries are precisely those who are benefitting most from today's deficits, it would remove a source of inequity for some taxpayers and could make the move to a PET easier to swallow politically.

[14] E. Cary Brown, "Business-Income Taxation and Investment Incentives," in Lloyd A. Metzler et al., *Income, Employment and Public Policy: Essays in Honor of Alvin M. Hansen,* Norton, New York, 1948. •

[15] This would require that taxes on negative net cash flow be refundable—that is, that the treasury would pay taxpayers with negative cash flow, or would carry losses over with interest.

[16] Aaron and Galper, in "Reforming the Tax System," have proposed a tax similar to the one described here and have also suggested that in order to prevent foreign holders of U.S. assets from escaping taxation, all cash distributions from corporations should be withheld at the top PET rate, with qualified accounts of U.S. taxpayers exempt from withholding.

[17] CBO, *Reducing the Deficit: Spending and Revenue Options,* Washington, D.C., February, 1984, p. 196.

[18] Henry J. Aaron (ed.), *The Value-Added Tax: Lessons from Europe,* The Brookings Institution, Washington, D.C., 1981, pp. 15-16. For a more positive recent discussion of the VAT, see Emil Sunley and Gerard Brannon, "Direct Consumption Taxes: Value Added and Retail Sales," in *Tax Policy: New Directions and Possibilities.*

CHAPTER SIX
THE BUDGET, POLITICS, AND THE CONSTITUTION

The preceding chapters have made a case that deficits of the size projected over the remainder of this decade will be harmful to long-term economic growth, while at the same time increasing the lifetime consumption of persons currently over age thirty. We have also made a case that reducing or eliminating the deficits will be no mean feat. Neither the spending nor revenue sides of the federal budget offer any easy fixes.

Having completed our purely economic analysis of the deficits, in this chapter we turn to the politics of the deficit reduction. Obviously, in one chapter we will not be able to provide a complete analysis of why it is that the deficits continue to be chosen as national policy, nor what forces might change current policy. However, neither the economics nor politics of the federal budget can be properly treated in isolation. They interact both in principle and in practice, and this chapter explores the major interactions. We deal here with two sets of questions:

1. Given the national concern about the prospective deficits, are there institutional changes, either at the legislative or constitutional levels, that should be made with a view to improving the ability of the federal government to take the long-term consequences of deficits into account?

2. Is it plausible that the economic costs of the prospective deficits can lead to a political consensus of sufficient power to implement a significant proportion of the tax and expenditure changes discussed in the preceding chapters?

Our discussion of procedural changes focuses on two: possible reforms in current budgetary practice, and a constitutional amendment to balance the budget.

At least the latter proposal now enjoys broad political support, having been endorsed by the Republican Party, the current President, and thirty-two state legislatures, two short of the number needed to call a constitutional convention on the issue.

Before turning to the budgetary process and the pros and cons or a constitutional amendment requiring budget balance, it is important to emphasize that the large current and prospective deficits are not accidents of the political process, but are considered policies chosen by the executive and legislative branches of the United States Government. While it is possible that changes in rules and procedures used in budgeting would lead to a reduction in future deficits, the only way that they can do so is by reducing spending or raising taxes. The "deficit problem" ultimately reflects the fact that the elimination of deficits is painful, requiring either major cuts in spending or in the after-tax income of citizens. This means that a constitutional amendment requiring budget balance does not solve the deficit problem; it merely requires that the problem be solved. The consequences of the solution— some combination of reduced federal spending and higher taxes—are just as painful, regardless of whether they are required by the Constitution or chosen in more conventional ways.

REFORM OF THE BUDGETARY PROCESS

If we were writing this book in the early 1970s, we would be tempted to argue that the size of the deficit was partly attributable to the fact that there existed no mechanism to require the Congress to look carefully at budget totals. Since the passage of the Budget Reform Act of 1974, however, it is very difficult to make the case that there is something amiss in the procedures that are used to arrive at a federal budget. Congress now has staff support available to it (through the two Budget Committees and the Congressional Budget Office) that is every bit as good as the staff support available to the Executive. Additionally, the Budget Act requires that Congress vote on budget totals, both for expenditures and for revenues, and makes it procedurally difficult to exceed these totals.[1] The Congressional budget process assures that the deficits we see are the deficits that were voted for. There is a mechanism to assure that the budget totals are considered, and they *are* considered. The President signs the spending bills. Thus it must be concluded that the budget deficit is chosen, as a matter of national policy, by those elected to make just such choices.

Most recent commentators on the deficit problem have taken pains to note that the budget process is not the culprit. Thus, for example, Alice Rivlin, who was director of the CBO for almost ten years, observes that "spending is no longer growing for the old pork barrel, log-rolling reasons. Prospective spending growth is concentrated in a small number of programs with very broad popular support (primarily defense, pensions, and medical benefits), and revenues after the tax changes in 1981 and 1982 are simply not growing fast enough to close the gap, even if the economy continues to improve. This is not a procedural problem, it is simply a question of wanting more government services than there are revenues to pay for them. . . ."[2] The new budget process has, to be sure, undergone some criticism.[3]

But this criticism is mainly of the efficiency type: The same results could be achieved with fewer hearings, fewer subcommittees, and less time. Be that as it may, the point here is that the current process does assure that deficits are not unintentional: The simple expedient of paying attention will not guarantee more responsible budget outcomes.

One potential reform of the budget process, championed by President Reagan, is the line-item veto. Under such a procedure, the President could accept all provisions in a spending bill—except a few—that he could strike with the line-item veto. Although the deficit problem is serious enough that anything may be worth a try, there are reasons for believing that this reform is unlikely to have much effect on the deficit. If the essential problem is that the society wants more from the federal government than it is willing to pay for, and there are no big-ticket items that are obvious targets for spending cuts, then there is little that the line-item veto can do. Moreover, forty-three states now have line-item vetoes, and they do not appear to behave very differently from the seven that do not. Their spending, when controlled or not controlled for other variables, is virtually the same as in states without a line-item veto. More interesting, from a political science perspective, is the fact that in a number of states the governor is forced to "cut a deal" with the legislature regarding how the line-item veto will be used in conjunction with the legislative approval of the budget.[4] In this case we find exactly what we would expect to find: That the politics of a problem manage to work their magic quite independently of the institutional rules. One would expect the same to be true at the federal level.

THE DEFICIT AND THE CONSTITUTION

In Chapters 1 and 2, we argued that there are times when deficits are helpful instruments of economic policy, and other times when the economic policy implied by deficits is a transfer of economic resources from the future to the present. The deficits currently in prospect for the remainder of this decade (and beyond) are of the latter sort. Current consumption will be increased at the expense of future consumption—and by "future consumption" we mean consumption very far in the future. Our best guess is that persons who expect to die in the next forty years will have their lifetime consumption increased by the deficits; those persons who are younger (including all of those persons yet to be born) will have reduced lifetime resources. The same analysis applies to changes in the deficit: Those older than thirty would gain from still larger deficits, while those younger than thirty would lose. In popular terms, running large deficits at times of high employment implies living off of capital; the larger the deficits, the higher the life in the short run, and the greater the future negative consequences in the longer run.

When framed in this way, the deficit indeed raises a constitutional issue: It is about the obligations of current citizens and the rights of younger citizens and citizens-to-be.[5] It will always be in the narrow self-interest of a majority of the voting age population to support policies that lead to deficits and consumption now at the expense of others' consumption later, and it may be necessary for a constitutional provision to prevent that. Indeed, all states except for Vermont now do try to prevent such overconsumption policies in their own state constitutions.

Of course, the constitutional issue is not the level of the deficit per se, but the extent to which those currently possessing political power are allowed to use the public sector to their own advantage relative to the advantage of those not yet on the scene. To complicate the problem, the deficit is not the only mechanism through which resources can be transferred across generations through public policy, and not all deficits make such a transfer. If, for example, deficits were occasioned by public capital investment, measures to boost private investment, or accompanied by increased protection of natural resources, there would be no violation of any implicit intergenerational obligation. Our discussion of economic growth isolated only one economic criterion of optimal fiscal behavior over time—that of overall economy-wide saving rates—not deficits per se. Hence while fiscal policy is potentially an appropriate subject for constitutional concern, it is extremely difficult to determine what the Constitution should say about measured budget deficits.

ARGUMENTS FOR AND AGAINST
A BALANCED BUDGET AMENDMENT

Armed with this philosophical ambiguity, we now examine some of the more technical problems that have been raised regarding a balanced budget amendment:

1. As we showed in Chapter 2, there are many times when a federal deficit is warranted as an instrument of economic policy. At times of low employment, the deficit makes it possible to increase demand and put otherwise idle resources to work, benefitting current citizens at no cost to future economic well-being, and perhaps adding to future well-being. A constitutional provision forbidding deficits, even if perfectly enforceable, would put the entire burden of macroeconomic stabilization onto monetary policy, leading to greater fluctuations in income, employment, the value of the dollar, and real interest rates.

    Of course, these fluctuations could be ameliorated if the amendment had an "escape clause." Under Resolution 58, a proposal for a balanced budget amendment that was passed by the Senate Judiciary Committee in 1981, a three-fifths majority of both houses could agree to suspend the requirement that the budget be in balance.[6] A requirement for a majority of this size means that deficits would be run only rarely, even when warranted. To reduce the requirement of a supernormal majority, on the other hand, would mean that the constitutional provision would have little effect.

2. The federal budget depends on forecasts. The budget for any fiscal year is proposed by the administration about eight months before the budget is to take effect. Even if it is enacted by the beginning of the fiscal year (a histor-

ical rarity), and if expenditives are on target (another rarity), revenues depend on GNP, which is difficult to forecast far ahead. Hence the economy will work its wonders on the budget for twenty months before all of the numbers are in. As a practical matter, then, it is impossible to assure that even a budget intended to be balanced in a given fiscal year, and adopted at the start of the fiscal year, will be in balance at the end of that year. Thus, a constitutional amendment requiring a balanced budget can, in practice, only require that the budget be forecast to be in balance. Budgeters can always generate forecasts that show budgets to be in balance, and it is easy to imagine Congress and the Administration producing prospectively "balanced" budgets based on forecasts that everyone knows to be highly implausible. The Court might then be called upon to judge whether the purposes of the Constitution were being achieved by such practice. This gives the amusing, but disquieting, prospect of judges evaluating politically motivated economic forecasts. This seems to be a long way from what the Constitution is supposed to be about.

3. There exist many "gimmicks" that can be used to get federal expenditures "off budget." We have discussed loan guarantees and the sales of federal assets. Sales of federal assets are counted as receipts, but from an economic standpoint, they should not be—they represent current usage of assets that could be held for the future. Loan guarantees and subsidies are ways in which the federal government can induce the private sector to engage in various activities, with roughly the same consequences as direct federal spending, but with small effect on the budget.[7] One can also imagine an increase in federal regulatory activity, requiring the private sector to undertake public functions, as another way of getting around a requirement for federal budget balance. A workable constitutional amendment would have to deal with all of these possibilities, and many more, requiring detailed technical language of a sort that appears nowhere else in the Constitution. In addition to making economic forecasts, we now have our Supreme Court justices engaging in budgetary accounting. Even if they do their job well, it is certain that not all possibilities will be included in any amendment, and so there will still be great potential for creative budgeting, with random, but surely inefficient, consequences for federal operations.

4. Recalling that the purpose of a balanced budget amendment, at least according to the logic of the argument we have made in this chapter, is to prevent the exploitation of future citizens, it would be appropriate to exempt a federal capital budget from limitation. That is, expenditures that had long periods of payoff could be appropriately financed at least partially by deficits, because those benefitting should also bear some costs. Indeed without such a provision, the balanced budget amendment could not come anywhere near to accomplishing the purpose of assuring intergenerational equity, which is its major justification. With such a provision, however, every program that the federal government operates would try to achieve "capital budget" status. Again, the Court would be required to determine what did and did not belong in the capital budget.

This is only part of the problem. To be consistent, our capital budget should exempt not only public capital formation from the deficit, but it *could* exempt grants to stimulate state and local capital formation and tax incentives for private investment, if these measures really did stimulate capital formation. Now our Supreme Court justices are into economic analysis.

5. A balanced budget amendment does nothing to solve the short-term difficulties that the budget cannot be balanced without cutting spending or increasing revenues. It is not enough to specify that budgets must be balanced: An amendment, or at least a procedure, must specify what changes are to be made if the budget is not balanced.

Therefore, although the deficit question does raise constitutional issues, the difficulties associated with implementing a balanced budget amendment that would prevent consumption binges at the expense of future generations seem far too great to make the effort worthwhile. There appears to be no workable method of embodying any agreed-upon notion of intergenerational equity into the Constitution. We also note (and later expand on the idea) that if there is general agreement on intergenerational equity, there exist legislative programs that would implement such agreement, and do so far more flexibly and responsibly than the Constitution could. We feel that those who are concerned about deficits should try to make that concern more politically salient than it seems to be currently, rather than seeking an essentially unworkable constitutional remedy. If a political consensus on the relevant issues can be reached, then the constitutional amendment is not needed. If the consensus cannot be reached, the constitutional amendment is likely to be ineffective in dealing with the longer-term consequences of deficits, but effective in adding further difficulties to what is already a cumbersome budgetary process.

POLITICS AND THE DEFICIT

At the beginning of this chapter, we noted that the deficit is a carefully considered and chosen national policy, not some accident of the way in which the federal budget is made. The reasons for this are clear enough—the set of things that the country views as being appropriate for the federal government to do costs more than the amount of revenue that people are willing to provide under the current tax system. Moreover, although the structural deficits themselves lead to much gnashing of teeth and public discussion, the fact is that the real economic costs of the deficits take place mostly in the future (in the present, real interest rates are high, but the effect on standards of living that arise from this occur, for the most part, only when those high real interest rates have had the time they need to reduce the capital stock); the real economic gains of not reducing federal spending or increasing federal taxes occur immediately.

From where, then, might come the political will to engage in policies that might lead to a substantial reduction in the structural federal deficit? There are basically three possibilities:

1. Voters and their elected representatives will articulate a view that short-term consumption is not what is most important, but that the state in which they leave economy for future generations matters to them, and that the deficit is a threat to the future well-being of persons whose welfare is of concern. Were this to come about, the consumption binge that is implied by the structural deficits would come to a halt, because the consumers themselves chose a different policy and became willing to cut spending and raise taxes.

2. High real interest rates and the strong dollar could affect enough people directly so that a political constituency for reducing the deficit could be built around these issues. This possibility seems unlikely, because the overall arithmetic of the timing of costs and benefits from deficit reduction still favors retaining the deficits—if current consumption is what people care about. Should a political constituency develop around these issues, it is more likely to be articulated around issues of protection from foreign competition (thus ameliorating the effects of the strong dollar) and special programs to diminish the effects of high real interest rates on home-buyers. Such policies could be targeted relatively effectively on those persons who are most directly affected by deficits in the short-term. Of course, adoption of such economically inefficient policies would reduce national wealth overall, and would do nothing about the long-term consequences of the deficits.

3. For some reason, possibly including (2) above, the deficit could bring about a crisis that demanded immediate political response. Note that the mere size and persistence of deficits has not by itself brought on such a crisis. One such crisis involves a credit crunch: Farmers (as in 1985) or less-developed countries (as in 1982) could experience income losses and have trouble meeting interest payments on their loans, and this could threaten the financial stability of commercial banks. Or, as the capital inflow to take advantage of high U.S. interest rates ceased, the dollar could start falling, leading to capital losses on U.S. securities, and to an accelerating decline. In the spring of 1980, the collapse of the long-term bond market, triggered by sharply rising interest rates, led quickly to both credit controls and a major round of budget cutting. It is possible that another such event could occur, and that the deficits would be seen as the culprit. Though panics and corrective measures are generally not well-grounded in real phenomena, there may be an "emergency" deficit reduction package. It is unlikely that such an emergency package will be optimal, as those who put the package together will have to act quickly; it seems bizarre to hope for a crisis to end a problem that should be corrected without a crisis.

If none of these scenarios occur, the United States will continue to run large deficits into the indefinite future, gradually reducing the wealth of the country but always preferring to have a little more to consume today rather than a little less for ourselves today and a little more for others tomorrow. Such an outcome does seem somewhat unlikely right now—plainly, there is great public unease about the large deficits. But it is always possible that if the crises do not occur—and they may not—society will simply learn to live with the deficits; and if so, it will always be in the narrow interest of a majority of voters to continue the policy.

We will not even attempt to speculate about which of these outcomes is the more likely. Our motive in writing the book is clearly to boost the chances of outcome (1). The whole issue could be put to rest, at least temporarily, by outcomes (2) or (3). Our main fear is that society will learn to enjoy its consumption binge, without fully recognizing the future costs that such an outcome will impose. Society may choose to have a consumption binge, but it should at least know the consequences of the choice.

NOTES

[1] After the adoption of the second budget resolution, just before the beginning of the fiscal year, any spending or revenue bill that would, in the opinion of the Budget Committees, cause the spending or revenue limits in the resolution to be violated cannot be considered.

[2] Alice M. Rivlin, "The Political Economy of Budget Deficits," *American Economic Review,* vol. 74, May, 1984, p. 137.

[3] See Alice M. Rivlin, *Economic Choices,* The Brookings Institution, Washing, D. C., 1984. See also Rudolph Penner (ed.), *The Congressional Budget Process after Five Years,* American Enterprise Institute, Washington, D.C., 1981.

[4] See U.S. House of Representatives, Committee on the Budget, "The Line Item Veto: An Appraisal," U.S. Government Printing Office, 1984.

[5] By "constitutional" we mean "pertaining to fundamental rights and obligations among members of the society," rather than pertaining to the Constitution as now written.

[6] Resolution 58 is at once a balanced budget amendment and a federal tax limitation amendment, making it even more unwieldy as a constitutional provision than would be the "generic" balanced budget amendment that we discuss here. Because our concern is with the deficit itself, and not the level of government spending, we do not provide an analysis of Resolution 58 in toto. For such an analysis, see Gardner Ackley, "You Can't Balance the Budget by Amendment," *Challenge,* vol. 25, November/December, 1982, pp. 4–13.

[7] For this reason, they should not be in NIA budgets, and are not. But "the budget" is the one written by politicians, not the NIA budget written by GNP accountants.

CHAPTER SEVEN
RECAPITULATION

The newspaper view of budget deficits appears to rest on three propositions:

1. Budget deficits are bad
2. The costs of budget deficits will become apparent very quickly
3. Budget deficits are easy to cut.

In the previous chapters we have attempted to argue against all three propositions. Our chapter on budgetary accounting (Chapter 1) suggests that it is not obvious what a properly measured budget deficit is, let alone whether it is good or not. Our chapter on macroeconomics (Chapter 2) argues that budget deficits are not always bad—sometimes a fiscal policy that yields budget deficits is the appropriate macroeconomic response to what would otherwise be a serious recession. It also argues that even if deficits are harmful in some sense, that sense is a very subtle one—with the true costs of the deficit sometimes not becoming apparent for many, many years. And our chapters on potential policy changes to correct deficits suggest that deficits are anything but easy to cure. Meaningful changes cannot be made by simply ferreting out waste, fraud, and abuse, but require significant policy changes with real political costs. Constitutional limits may force the job to be done, but they will not do it; they are difficult to write sensibly, and they also entail other costs.

All of this suggests a few broad lessons. The first, and probably most fundamental, is that simple shibboleths will not do. Serious decisions about fiscal policy require serious analyses of the issues and a willingness to compromise on certain goals, whether they be social, economic, or political, for the sake of accomplishing other objectives. It is not productive to have politicians oppose realistic efforts to correct budget deficits, offering as an excuse the fact that they have favored constitutional remedies. It is not productive to rely on efforts to locate and cut the fat out of government as a way to stop deficits—the fat that can be trimmed without making difficult political choices is far from sufficient to do the job. And it is no more productive to claim that taxes on the rich will do the job. To do the job will require higher taxes on a great many people.

The second important general lesson involves the nature of the real costs of deficit spending. There have been so many scare stories trying to impugn deficits, often inappropriately, that people can be forgiven for their confusion in understanding the issue. For that reason, we have attempted to emphasize (no doubt some would say *belabor*) the point that the real costs involve a massive reduction in investment for the American economy. The reduced investment may be at the expense of capital that would otherwise be located in this country; it may siphon off capital that would otherwise be located in poorer countries abroad. Either way, it will hurt future living standards, in this country and abroad, in a way that we find indefensible. When we refer to deficits by the pejorative term "consumption binge," we mean exactly that.

The third important general lesson deals with the time dimension. Time is either short or long, depending on the issue. To correct the deficit, time is short, in the sense that federal interest obligations are building up year by year. The longer fiscal responsibility is postponed, the greater the costs become. In this policy sense, the United States is definitely confronted with what we have called a "ticking time bomb." But there is another sense in which the relevant time horizon is very long. The true costs of deficits do not come until far in the future, when years and perhaps decades of reduced investment show up in the form of lower living standards, which by then become inescapable. The right way to think about deficits, then, is to have a sense of urgency about acting now, because of what one knows will happen far into the future.

Beyond these general lessons, each chapter in this book deals with more technical points—which also might bear repeating. The underlying theme of the chapter on accounting (Chapter 1) is that the government conducts many different types of transactions with the private sector, and for that reason it is not easy to record its transactions in a summary measure that will be appropriate for all purposes. In line with our feeling that the important reason for keeping track of government fiscal measures in the long run is just the capital formation issue, we have tried to walk through the various accounting concepts with this focus. Although the official deficit is not always appropriate from this capital formation standpoint, and although deficits should have been measured in a more refined way during many past epochs, the interesting thing about the deficits forecast for the balance of the 1980s is that accounting does not matter much. No matter how one counts, one gets the same answer—deficits are going to be enormous, and this seems likely to be bad for capital formation.

The chapter on macroeconomics (Chapter 2) retains the capital formation focus, this time to show how one might evaluate the deficits and the expansionary fiscal policy that they usually imply. There is, first of all, an important difference between the short run, when it is realistic to assume that the economy's productive capacity is fixed and full employment is not guaranteed, and the long run, when there should be reasonably high levels of employment but when the economy's productive capacity and standard of living are not fixed. For fifty years now most economists have agreed that there are cases when deficit spending does make sense in the short run—it can improve employment prospects without worsening long-run living standards. We support, and try to give arguments in favor of, this position. Such arguments imply that the large budget deficits run in years such as 1975 (by President Ford) and 1982 (by President Reagan) were generally appropriate.

At the same time, deficits are not always appropriate, and there are cases when deficit spending involves costs in both the short and the long term. The short-term costs may be in the form of excess stimulation of employment, leading to increased price inflation; the long-term costs may be in the form of reduced capital formation. Although both are serious, the capital formation costs are far more serious, and irreparable. We foresee these costs in the enormous deficits forecast of the 1980s, and for that reason wish them to be reduced. In our view there is no question that these future deficits now represent the most serious issue confronting U.S. economic policy makers.

The chapter on interest payments (Chapter 3) can almost be regarded as a digression, and it has a very simple point—the longer the country waits to correct its deficits, the more costly the corrections will be, because of the steady accretion of interest obligations. If there is ever a case for "cold turkey" remedies, the United States seems to have one here.

The long chapter on measures to reduce the deficit by curbing spending (Chapter 4) is perhaps the most pessimistic chapter in the book. Most people think that there is a lot of fat in government spending—fat that is easy to cut out. The hard truth seems to be that neither proposition is correct. Interest payments, a high and rising share of total spending, cannot be cut at all in the short run. Social security benefits, another high and rising share, cannot be made permanently lower without making revenues also permanently lower, having essentially no effect on the long-run deficit. Defense spending can be cut, but the major cuts involve buying fewer weapons of one sort or another, and hence real policy tradeoffs. There are also a host of cutbacks involving lesser ticket items, but even though these potential cutbacks would save less money, they imply political antagonisms that may be every bit as large—farm price supports cannot be cut without making farmers mad, revenue sharing cannot be cut without making mayors mad, and so forth. There are cuts that can be made, but if it were easy to make the cuts, or if there were general agreement to make them, they would have been made already.

The chapter on taxes (Chapter 5) is perhaps slightly more optimistic, because at least there are ways of raising taxes enough to eliminate the deficit. The trick is that the overall federal tax base must be broadened. That in turn can be done through the introduction of new tax sources, such as a national retail sales tax or a value-added tax, by broadening the base of the personal income tax, the current Congressional favorite, or by replacing the personal income tax with a broad-based and progressive expenditure tax, our own favorite. The costs and benefits of each of these measures can and have been debated extensively—as always, nothing is perfect—but the fundamental truism must always be kept in mind. Taxes are hard to raise without introducing new tax distortions and new political antagonisms. There is a tax change route to curing deficits, but it is likely to entail some economic and even more political costs.

Chapter 6 talks about deficit cutting from a more procedural standpoint. Is there a point in changing the way Congress and the President determine fiscal policy, as opposed to the particulars of fiscal policy? Again, we incline toward the pessimistic. One reason is historical. Congress has already tried to change procedures once, in the 1974 Congressional Budget Act. Some good did come from the measure, for now there is at least a way of providing impartial data and an explicit procedure for reconciliation of fiscal discrepancies. But some high deficits came out of the procedure, too, as witnessed by the present figures. The underlying truth is that if there is not the political will to correct deficits, procedures alone will not be enough. Based on this truth, we are skeptical that a constitutional limit on deficit spending could even correct the deficits, and there are massive problems of definition and implementation with such measures. Moreover, if the limits should happen to work, some of those good deficits we just spoke about go down the drain. Although there might be some form of structural limitation that would impede the ability of Congresses and Presidents to go on consumption binges, the better solution would be to make that a part of the accepted unwritten American constitution.

It all adds up to a sober picture. We find great long-run harm in the deficits, yet we see no easy way to avoid them.

DESCRIPTION
OF KEY TERMS

Throughout this book, we have attempted to avoid unnecessary economic jargon, partly because we find such language to be ugly, and partly because we wish to be accessible to people who have managed to lead full lives without taking economics courses, or at least without having taken them lately. There are a number of elements of the economist's lexicon, however, that are very useful—and that save a lot of orotund prose. In the interest of economy, then, we do use some of these terms, and here provide a brief guide to those terms of art that appear below. Readers who have had the misfortune of formal training in the field may skip the following discussion without penalty.

Flows Many economic variables, such as GNP, investment, the deficit, supply, and demand, are measured as amounts of something per unit of time. Usually the unit of time is a year, though it could also be a month, quarter, or half-year. Thus, when we say that the deficit is $185 billion, we mean that it is $185 billion per year. As a general matter, when we discuss current activities, especially production, consumption, and investment, we are talking about flows, and unless we say otherwise, we are talking about flows per year.

Stocks In contrast to flows, which occur over some defined time period, stocks are simply quantities of stuff in existence. Thus we often refer to the *national capital stock*, which is the total amount of equipment and structures that exist at some time. We also refer to the *total national debt*, which is the total quantity of interest-bearing financial liabilities on the federal government's balance sheet. The *deficit* is flow that adds to the stock of debt, just as *investment* is a flow that adds to the capital stock. If the deficit were to be eliminated, the debt would stop growing, but it would not shrink. Similarly, if all new investment were to be halted, the capital stock that currently existed would still exist, although it would gradually get smaller as it experienced physical depreciation.

Net and Gross Investment The wearing out of the capital stock is called *depreciation* (a flow). In order simply to maintain the size of the capital stock, annual depreciation of capital stock must be replaced, through new investment, in each year. In recent years, depreciation of the private nonresidential capital stock has been about 10 percent of GNP, implying that 10 percent of GNP must be devoted to nonresidential investment in each year just to keep the capital stock constant. In order for the capital stock to increase, investment must exceed 10 percent of GNP. The excess of investment over depreciation is called *net investment*; the total amount of investment is called *gross investment*. Net investment is the key variable in economic growth—it determines how rapidly living standards will rise. Gross investment, the total amount of new machinery, equipment, and structures put in place in a given year, is a key component of GNP in itself, and is very important in short-term analysis of national income and outcome. Thus, both concepts are important, but they are important for different issues—net investment for long-term living standards, and gross investment for short-term economic activity.

Cyclical, trend, the long run, and short run Over *very* long periods of time (five years or more) the performance of the economy on average will be determined by its productive capacity, or potential GNP. Thus over the long run, we are interested in the trend growth of potential output, the amount that would be produced at some given and fairly high level of resource utilization. In the shorter run, the economy may operate either below or above potential. In the former case, there is substantial unemployment, and in the latter case, inflation tends to accelerate. These deviations from potential GNP are referred to as *cyclical*, in that they are a product of the business cycle, rather than long-term trends. Note that the business cycle is something of a misnomer, because its amplitude and period are both highly variable. However, the term has been in use for the better part of a century, and if it is interpreted to be synonymous with deviations from trend, and to connote relatively short-term (anything between a calendar quarter and two calendar years) phenomena, it is a useful term of art, and we have used it.

Real and Nominal Most of the economic variables we discuss are measured in dollars, and one of the truisms of modern life is that the value of a dollar falls over time because of inflation. In order to make comparisons across different time periods, then, economists adjust for the fact that prices in general have been rising, and often measure things in real or constant dollars. Thus, if prices overall have roughly doubled since 1974, it takes twice as many dollars now to buy the same amount of real stuff as it did then. GNP (the value of all things produced in 1984) is currently 3.66 trillion dollars. In 1974 it was 1.43 trillion. Thus nominal GNP rose by 155 percent. But because prices rose by 94 percent, real GNP, the actual physical amount of goods that the economy produced, rose by only 32 percent over the period. For most purposes, real variables are measured according to the value of dollars in 1972. And, for most purposes, real variables are the ones that are of most significance.

Real and Nominal Interest Rates One important application of the distinction between real and nominal quantities involves interest rates. Because cash balances pay zero interest, the interest rate can be thought of as the price of holding cash for a year. The real interest rate is the market interest rate less the rate of inflation. Thus, if inflation is 5 percent per year, and the cost of borrowing is 8 percent, the real interest rate is 3 percent. If one borrows a dollar at 8 percent and buys an average commodity with it, its value will rise 5 percent (the rate of inflation) over the next year. Similarly, if one lends a dollar at 8 percent, one anticipates that next year everything will cost 5 percent more, so the net return from making the loan is only 3 percent. Thus, the real cost of borrowing (real return from lending) is only 3 percent, the total cost less the anticipated appreciation of any real commodity that might be bought next year by either the creditor or lender. The real interest rate then becomes a much better measure of borrowing costs than the nominal rate, and this is one case where popular usage is very different from economists' usage. Since 1981, nominal interest rates have fallen sharply, while real rates have risen. This has happened because inflation has fallen even more than nominal rates have. Thus the true economic cost of borrowing has gone up, even as the dollar cost of borrowing a given amount of money has fallen.

Indexing   Indexing simply refers to a method of adjusting for the consequences of price changes, so that economic transactions take place in real terms, rather than nominal ones. When contracts are indexed, the consequences of inflation are removed. There are a number of examples, the most important of which is the indexing of social security payments. Every year, social security payments are increased to keep the value of any individual's pension constant in real terms. The nominal amount of the checks written is increased by the rate of inflation in consumer prices. Similarly, under the 1981 Economic Recovery Tax Act, the entire personal income tax structure is indexed such that if an individual's income rises at the rate of inflation, her income tax liability will rise by the same proportion but not by any more, as it would have when the progressive income tax was not indexed. Finally, one might imagine loans that are indexed. Jones might agree to lend Smith $1000 over four years, with the interest rate changing every year so as to make the real interest rate 3 percent per year. In this case, Smith would pay Jones 3 percent of $1000 plus the rate of inflation times $1000 every year.

Elasticity   Elasticity refers to the responsiveness of the supply or demand for commodities to changes in their prices. The more responsive, the more elastic. That is, if the supply of loanable funds to the U.S. government is very elastic, it means that small changes in the interest rate will lead to large changes in the volume of funds available. If the supply is inelastic, the interest rate would have to rise substantially in order to yield much of an increase in the supply of funds. As a general matter, the internationalization of economies makes supplies of things more elastic, because it is now possible to obtain them from foreign as well as domestic sources. This fact is used often in the discussion particularly when we discuss "open" economy macroeconomics and whether the government debt should be viewed as internal or external.

Open and Closed Economies   As the previous sentence suggested, an open economy is one where sales and purchases of goods and capital to and from foreigners are important. A closed economy is one where they are ignored. Until recently, most U.S. macroeconomics was taught as closed economy macroeconomics. Nowadays it should be taught as open economy macroeconomics, for the simple reason that the U.S. economy behaves very much like an open economy. Here we do a bit of both, using the open economy model whenever its lessons are important.

Portfolios   An individual's portfolio of assets is simply the types of assets that she holds. As a general matter, people will want some diversity of assets—some cash, some government bonds, some bank accounts, some stocks, one's own house, and so on. As rates of return and risk of different types of assets change, so too will portfolio composition, and one of the issues with which we deal in this book is the way in which portfolios might change as the stock of public debt changes and as interest rates change in response to deficits.

Marginal Product of Capital Imagine a machine that is worth one dollar, wears out (depreciates) at 10 percent per year, and, when operated efficiently, generates output worth 15 percent of its value each year. The machine is part of the capital stock, and the gross marginal product of the machine (the output generated when this machine is placed in use) is 15 percent, whereas the net marginal product (deducting the depreciation, which causes the machine to lose real value) is 5 percent per year. We will often refer simply to the *marginal product of capital*, by which we mean the net marginal product, the amount of output produced per unit of capital after depreciation has been recovered. Note that the net marginal product of capital should be roughly equal for all types of capital in use. If this were not the case, people would adjust their portfolios toward those types of capital that had the highest net marginal product (exactly the net return per dollar of saving), and the law of diminishing returns would drive the return on the highest-yield assets down to the point where all assets had about the same yield. Thus it is roughly correct (subject to all sorts of caveats that appear in the text) to refer to *the* marginal product of capital in general, and we make such reference in the text.

The same logic implies that the net marginal product of capital should be roughly equal to the real interest rate. If it were not, firms could expand profits by borrowing, buying capital goods, and producing. They would do this until the supply of capital had expanded enough that its net marginal product is driven down to the real interest rate. At that point the famous market signal tells firms to stop investing—now the economy is in capital market equilibrium.

The concept of the marginal product of capital also makes it easier to talk about tax policy. We favor a tax system that taxes all forms of capital evenly, hence leading to no impact on the allocation of capital. If this were not the case, the marginal product of capital would be driven up in a heavily taxed activity (to compensate for the tax) and down in other activities. Total output could be increased simply by reallocating the capital to the high-product activity until the marginal products were equal, or by making the tax system neutral.

Economic Rent Economic rent, as distinct from apartment rent, is a payment to any owner or producer that exceeds what would be necessary to get the owner or producer to provide his or her product. Thus, when Willie Stargell says he loves baseball so much he would play it for nothing, his entire salary can be considered economic rent. An example, more relevant for this book, is when a capital asset turns out to be unexpectedly productive, and earns more than the general rate of return to capital, the extra returns to the asset are considered economic rent. The remarkable thing about economic rent is that it can be taxed without affecting the allocation of resources. Even if Mr. Stargell had to pay higher income tax (and we take him at his word), he would have played just as much baseball. If an asset that turns out to be especially valuable earns a supernormal rate of return, a tax on the excess return (the rent) will not affect its use, because a similar asset can be produced at cost, and the excess return over cost is not needed in order to induce the asset to be produced and used.

Tax Arbitrage   Arbitrage is a central idea in microeconomic theory. Basically, it is the ancient practice of buying cheap and selling dear. When the economy provides opportunities for such practice, someone will engage in it, up to the point where the price of the commodity where it is cheap is bid up, and that where it is dear is bid down (due to enhanced supply), so that there is no price difference left to take advantage of. We rarely observe cases where similar commodities command different prices precisely because when such cases arise there is money to be made through arbitrage, and in a market economy the opportunity will be taken.

When different types of investment face different rates of tax, there will be tax arbitrage. Investors are concerned with their after-tax rates of return, and will invest in different assets until these are equalized. The simultaneous presence of tax-free investment opportunities (e.g., IRAs and tax-free municipal bonds) and the deductibility of interest leads to situations in which a taxpayer can borrow at (say) 14 percent, deduct the interest on his loan, and invest tax free at (say) 10 percent. The taxpayer gets a tax-free return of 3 percent a year merely by shifting assets around, with no net increase in economy-wide savings. Hence the whole point of the elimination of tax on the IRA has been subverted. In this case, the activity will not occur to the point where rates of return are equalized because there is a limit to the degree to which taxpayers can invest tax free.

In general, whenever assets are moved around solely to take advantage of the fact that different assets receive different tax treatment, there is tax arbitrage. If the tax system treated all capital income in the same way, there would be no such opportunities.

APPENDIX A
IS AND LM CURVES

In this appendix we examine more carefully the process by which investment gets "crowded out" by government deficits. The analysis uses a graphical apparatus for explaining the Keynesian system first developed by John R. Hicks, and named the IS–LM analysis.[1]

The IS–LM diagram is shown in Fig. A.1. On the horizontal axis is the level of real GNP, here called Y; on the vertical axis is the level of real interest rates, here called r. It is important to remember that this diagram works entirely in terms of real variables. It is normally used to understand the impact of short-run movements in output and interest rates following a monetary or fiscal change, in which case prices are assumed fixed (as described in the text) and there is no difference between nominal and real changes. We also use it here to see what happens to output and interest rates in the long run following a government budget deficit, in which case there is a difference, and our graph should be interpreted in real terms.

There are two important curves, or relationships, shown. One curve gives the set of points that brings the market for real output into equilibrium. This set of points is called the *IS curve* because in output equilibrium investment equals saving (as we have discussed in the text). The other curve gives the set of points that brings the money market into equilibrium. This set is called the *LM curve* because in equilibrium the demand for money, often called L, equals its supply, M.

Taking up the IS curve first, this curve assumes that basic spending demands, taxes, and government purchases are given, and shows how real output changes when interest rates change. If, for example, they drop, everything remains the same except that the return on financial assets is lower, and firms should therefore make more capital investment. As falling interest rates stimulate more capital investment, this investment raises real output (just as we showed in Fig. 2.1 on page 19), and

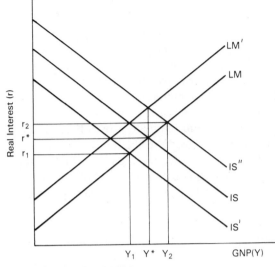

FIGURE A.1 IS and LM Curves.

the curve slopes downward. Lower real interest rates generate higher real output in the market for real output.⌉

Changes in real interest rates cause movements along the IS curve. What shifts the IS curve are changes in the basic spending propensities held in the background. If, for example, there were an autonomous fall in investment demand, there would be less investment and less real output at every level of r, and the IS curve would shift down to IS'.⌊If, on the other hand, the government ran a deficit by either cutting taxes or raising purchases, there would be more real output at every level of r and the IS curve would shift out to IS".⌋

The reasoning is very similar for the LM curve, except that now we are equilibrating the money market. The LM curve assumes that the "Fed" fixes the nominal supply of money, and that the forces that determine the underlying transactions demand for money are also fixed. If output were to rise, households would need more money to conduct their higher level of transactions, and the demand for money would rise. If the "Fed" is fixing supply, there is only one thing that can happen—the price, or opportunity cost, of holding money must rise to induce people to hold just the fixed supply. This opportunity cost of holding money is just the interest rate, what a household receives if it holds assets other than currency. Once this interest rate rises, the demand for money again equals its fixed supply. This means that as far as the money market is concerned, the LM curve slopes up ⌊A higher output leads to more transactions demand for money, and then to higher interest rates to clear the money market.⌋

Changes in real output cause a movement along the LM curve, and changes in the money supply shift it. Suppose there is no change in real output but the "Fed" reduces the supply of money. Then interest rates must rise, just as before. In this case, higher interest rates go along with each level of output, and the LM curve shifts up to LM'.

The IS curve gives the whole set of points that clear the market for real output; the LM curve gives the whole set of points that clear the money market. When the two curves are plotted together, we can find the one point on both curves that simultaneously clears both the market for real output and the money market. This point is obviously the intersection between the two curves. To go along with the story told in Chapter 2 of the text, we have drawn this intersection as occurring just at the high employment level of output, Y^*, and interest rates, r^*.

The first case examined in the text is where investment suddenly drops. As can now be readily seen, this drop implies a shift in the IS curve to IS', and a drop in both Y and r to Y_1 and r_1, respectively. Something like this happens in recessions, which are characterized by drops in both real output and real interest rates. To prevent Y from dropping through stabilization policy, the government can run a deficit. This deficit shifts out the IS curve and keeps Y and r much closer to their initial values.

Now suppose that investment did not drop, but that the government ran a deficit anyway. This is the second situation described in the text, and indeed close to what is happening now in the United States. In this event, the IS curve would shift up to IS'' and both Y and r would rise to Y_2 and r_2. The rise in r would immediately "crowd out" some real investment that would otherwise have been made, and in this sense is bad for capital formation. (Contrast the situation with the previous case, where deficits are used to respond to a drop in investment that would have occurred anyway.) But in the long run the crowding-out problem is even more serious because the output in excess of high employment levels eventually stimulates rising prices. If the "Fed" holds constant the stock of money in nominal terms, which is more or less what it will do, the real stock falls, and the LM curve gradually shifts up to LM'. In the long run real output returns to its initial value, Y^*, but interest rates are higher for two reasons, short-run and long-run crowding out. It stands to reason that capital investment will be lower for these two reasons also. In this case the deficits have not raised GNP, but they have caused some inflation, they have raised real interest rates greatly, and they have crowded out a greal deal of capital investment.

Finally, we examine how these curves react when economies are open to international trade and capital flows, and when exchange rates are flexible. Take the case of expansionary fiscal policy first. Initially, that shifts the IS curve to IS''. The rise in U.S. interest rates makes dollar-denominated securities relatively more attractive than those in other countries and attracts foreign investment funds to the United States. As foreign investors convert their funds to U.S. assets, the demand for dollars relative to foreign currency rises, and the dollar rises in value. This makes it harder for domestic exporters to sell their goods abroad, harder for domestic manufacturers to compete with imports, and lowers the net exports component of the IS curve. In the extreme case, U.S. interest rates cannot permanently stay above foreign interest rates (here r^*). Hence the drop in net exports shifts the IS curve all the way back to IS, and GNP all the way back to Y^*. There is crowding out, as before, but it happens much more quickly. Government deficits are now accompanied by high dollar values and a falling trade balance, exactly as has happened in the United States recently. In this case fiscal expansion does not lower the physical stock of capital located in the United States, but it does lower the amount U.S. citizens own. Hence it lowers future U.S. income just as if physical investment had been crowded out.

NOTES

[1] John R. Hicks, "Mr. Keynes and the Classics: A Suggested Interpretation," *Econometrica*, vol. 5, April, 1937, pp. 147-159.

APPENDIX B
THE NEOCLASSICAL
GROWTH MODEL

Here we examine more carefully the process by which changes in an economy's aggregate saving rate (the sum of private and governmental saving) translate into a level of capital stock and standard of living. The analysis is based on what is known as a *neoclassical growth model*, generally following a series of articles by Robert M. Solow.[1]

The basic assumptions made in the neoclassical growth model are described in the text:

1. Because of the long-term flexibility of prices and wages, output is assumed to equal its full employment level
2. Because output is at its full employment level, the share of output invested every year equals the share saved by the private and public sector
3. Because of competition among investors, the marginal product of capital is driven down to the real interest rate.

Although one could do the analysis for open economies with flexible exchange rates and mobile international capital, and arrive at similar conclusions, we show here just the closed economy case.

All of these new assumptions are embodied in the neoclassical growth model diagrammed by Fig. B.1. The figure is entirely in per worker terms, comparing output per worker (y, with the lowercase letters referring to a variable divided by the number of workers) to the stock of capital per worker, or the capital-labor ratio (k).

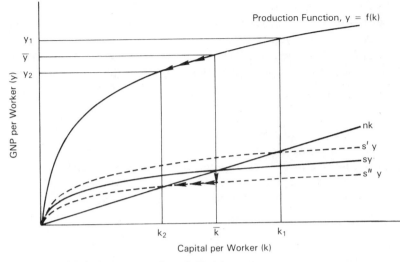

FIGURE B.1 The Neoclassical Growth Model.

Three important relationships are shown in Fig. B.1. The top line, labeled a *production function*, graphs the relationship between output and capital per worker. As capital per worker expands, output per worker does, too, though at diminishing rates because of the famous law of diminishing returns. The slope of this production function, representing the change in output per unit change in capital, is just the marginal product of capital. In the long run covered by this chart, we can expect that firms will invest until this marginal product of capital equals the real interest rate defined in Chapter 1. In this equilibrium, firms should be indifferent between spending a dollar more on capital, on which they earn its marginal product, and on financial assets, on which they make the real interest rate.

The second important relationship is the saving schedule, sy. This saving schedule refers to the sum of public and private saving discussed already, except that saving is converted to a proportion, s, of output. If the share s of all output is saved (through the investment-saving identity) and devoted to capital formation, sy then determines the amount of per-worker output used to build up the nation's capital stock in any year.

The third important relationship, added to Fig. B.1 to allow us to determine equilibrium values, is called the *capital requirements function*. It shows nothing more than the amount of output that must be devoted to capital formation to hold the capital–labor ratio at its initial value. Suppose the initial capital–labor ratio is k_0, and the labor force is growing at the rate of n per year. The nk_0 of new output must be used to equip all new workers with capital at the prevailing average rate to keep the capital–labor ratio the same. If the capital–labor ratio were 5 (every worker had 5 machines, valued in terms of output prices), there were 100 workers, and the labor force was growing at 2 percent per year, $5*0.02 = 0.1$ per worker must be devoted to new machines to give the 2 new workers their 5 machines apiece and keep the overall capital–labor ratio constant.

In equilibrium the economy will settle at the point of intersection where the saving curve equals the requirements line. The formula for this equilibrium solution is

$$sy = nk \qquad\qquad (1)$$

Using actual values, suppose that output was 100 and there were 100 workers in this economy, making for a level of output per worker equal to 1. As in the above example, if n were 0.02, this economy would have 2 new workers a year. If k were 5, the economy would need 10 new machines to equip the new workers at the prevailing capital–labor ratio. Then suppose that the share of output devoted to capital formation was 0.1. Every year this economy would create exactly the 10 new machines—both sy and $nk = 0.1$. The equation would be fulfilled, and the economy would be on an equilibrium growth path. The labor force would be growing at rate n on this path, and the capital stock would be, too, so that the capital–labor ratio would be stable at k. Total output would grow at rate n, too, so that output per worker would be stable at y.

Now suppose everything is the same except that 0.15 of new output is devoted to capital formation. Using Equation (1), the economy now produces 15 new machines a year to equip the 2 new workers. The higher saving rate (s') thus equips the new workers with more capital than the old workers, and eventually causes the economy's capital–labor ratio to rise to k_1 .[2] If, on the other hand, the saving rate were to fall, the capital–labor ratio would, too. These growth models then show how the share of output devoted to capital formation ultimately determines the economy's capital–labor ratio.

These examples seem to imply that it is always better to save more, because saving always raises the economy's capital–labor ratio. But such is not the case. In these models, increased saving is desirable to the extent that it raises the capital–labor ratio and equips workers with more capital, but it has a cost, too, in that workers must forego consumption to yield this additional capital. To take an extreme example, it would be foolish for a society to devote all of its output to saving, because consumption per capita would always be zero in such an economy.

This puzzle raises the question of whether there is an optimal saving rate for an economy. Under a number of strong assumptions, that can be found using the same simple growth model, following an analysis of Edmund Phelps.[3] The first step in this analysis is to note that in equilibrium for a constant saving ratio, consumption equals the difference between the y line and the nk line. The former sets the equilibrium output of an economy, and the latter sets the equilibrium level of saving—with the difference then being equilibrium consumption per worker. In the above example, when output per worker is 1 and the saving rate is 0.1, equilibrium consumption per worker is 0.9. As with the other variables, gross consumption grows at rate n, and per-worker consumption is stable in this equilibrium.[4]

The optimal saving rate for the economy might then be defined as that saving rate that maximizes the level of consumption per worker over time. This is just the same as maximizing the difference between the y line and the nk line, or of finding the point on the y line where its slope equals the slope of the nk line. To avoid diagrammatic "clutter," these points are drawn as k_1 and y_1 in Fig. B.1. The slope of the y line is the marginal product of capital, or the real interest rate. The slope of the nk line is simply n (note that the change in the vertical axis per unit of k is just nk). The optimal point is found where $r = n$. A bit of algebra can also show that this optimal point can also be found in terms of the share of output devoted to capital formation.[5]

It can be shown that the United States and most other countries are now saving much less than the share of output needed to maximize consumption levels over time.[6] One can have a deep, and irresolvable, debate about whether countries should up their saving rate for this reason. After all, increased saving would represent a sacrifice of consumption goods by those living now for the sake of those living later—and those living later would, in general, already have higher living standards. Countries would in effect be having permanent industrial revolutions. Without getting into this question, it is still helpful to know the optimal saving rate as defined above, because it tells whether changes in the saving rate will raise or lower future consumption levels, or future living standards. For the United States, there appears to be little question that saving less now will lead ultimately to lower per capita consumption levels than would otherwise be the case.

The analysis of the long-term impact of government deficits follows in straightforward fashion. We have already established that deficits not occasioned by public capital formation or offset by private saving increases can be viewed as dissaving, in that they lower the economy's share of output devoted to capital formation. The growth analysis now shows how deficits, if maintained over time, will ultimately lower the economy's capital–labor ratio and level of consumption per capita. Beginning with a position of budget balance and a capital–labor ratio of k, if the economy depicted in Fig. B.1 were to run deficits, it would find its aggregate saving rate reduced to s", its capital–labor ratio to k_2, and its per capita level of output to y_2. The growth process of the economy would follow the path indicated by the arrows. At first the deficits would simply represent a drop in s at the initial k value. Because k is the same, y is the same—and the drop in the share of output devoted to capital formation implies a rise in the share of output devoted to consumption; this economy is on a consumption binge. But eventually the policy will hurt consumption—the lower saving rate will not be sufficient to maintain the k level; the economy's capital–labor ratio must fall to k_2; and output and consumption will fall along with it. In the new equilibrium, as in the old, everything will be growing at rate n, but the economy will have less capital per worker, less output per worker, and lower living standards.

NOTES

[1] Robert M. Solow, "A Contribution to the Theory of Economic Growth," *Quarterly Journal of Economics*, vol. 70, February, 1956, pp. 65–94.

[2] Using the identity $sy = nk$, it would seem that a rise in s from 0.1 to 0.15 would raise k from 5 to 7.5. But alas, the model is not quite that simple, because as k rises, y rises as well. The true equilibrium value of k would then be larger than 7.5.

[3] In Edmund S. Phelps, "The Golden Rule of Accumulation: A Fable for Growthmen," *American Economic Review*, vol. 51, September, 1961, pp. 638–643.

[4] This may appear to be a discouraging conclusion—all this investment and living standards (consumption per capita) do not even rise? In fact, living standards *can* rise, once the population growth term is broadened to include workers released from old machines by technological progress.

[5] The algebra is as follows. In equilibrium, $sy = nk$. Consumption is maximized when $r = n$. Substituting, we have $s = nk/y = rk/y$. The latter ratio is just the share of returns to capital in total output. Hence an alternative way of stating the optimal saving proposition is that the share of output devoted to capital formation, s, should equal the share of returns to capital.

[6] To show it is a bit complicated. A paper that deals with the ins and outs of the demonstration is Edward M. Gramlich, "How Bad Are the Large Deficits?", in Greg B. Mills and John L. Palmer (eds.), *Budget Policy in the Reagan Administration*, The Urban Institute, Washington, D.C., 1984.

INDEX